MOVING ...

A Complete Checklist and Guide for Relocation

by Karen G. Adams

Silvercat Publications
San Diego, California

10 9 8 7 6 5 4 3 2 1

Cover art by Keith Adams.

Library of Congress Cataloging-in-Publication Data

Adams, Karen G., 1953-
    Moving : a complete checklist and guide for relocation / by
Karen G. Adams
            p.   cm.
    Includes bibliographical references.
    ISBN 0-9624945-6-9 : $8.95
    1. Moving, Household. I. Title.
TX307-A33   1994
648'.9--dc20   94-10068
                                                        CIP

Printed in the United States of America

Contents

Introduction   **5**

Part 1: Planning Your Move   **9**
 A. Preparation 9
  If You Are Selling Your House 10
 B. Budgeting 12
 C. A House-Hunting Trip 14
 D. A Professional Move 17
 E. A Do-It-Yourself Move 21
 F. Packing Tips 23
  Some Important Pointers For Lifting 25
 G. Insurance 27
 H. Business, Finance, And Attractions 28
 I. Address Labels 30
 J. Moving with a Pet 32

Part 2: Six to Eight Weeks before You Move **35**
 A Sorting Through Your Belongings 35
 B. Holding A Garage Sale 36
 C. Making an Inventory and a List of Shipments 38
 D. Considering Storage 40
 E. Household Tasks 41
 F. Business, Finance, And Attractions 42

Part 3: Four and Five Weeks before You Move **45**
 A. Starting To Clean 45
 B. Taking A Food Inventory 47
 C. Household Tasks 48
 D. Business, Finance, And Attractions 49

Part 4: Two and Three Weeks before You Move **51**
 A. Preparations 51
 B. Household Tasks 53
 C. Business, Finance, And Attractions 54
 D. Garage, Patio, And Outdoor Equipment 56
 E. Food, Plants, Liquor 58
 F. Friends And Acquaintances 59

Part 5: One Week Before You Move **61**
 A. Cleaning 61
 B. Household Tasks 62
 C. Starting To Pack 63
 D. Children And Pets 64

Part 6: One and Two Days before You Move   65
  A. Organizing And Packing 65
  B. Appliances And Electronic Equipment 66
  C. Yardwork And Outdoor Equipment 68
  D Household Tasks 69
  E. Last Minute Arrangements 71

Part 7: Professional Packing And Moving   73
  A. Preparations 73
  B. Instructions for Packers and Movers 75
  C. Inventory Sheets 77
  D. Loading 78
  E. Before The Movers Leave 80
  F. After The Movers Leave 82

Part 8: Arriving At Your Destination   83
  A. First Things 83
  B. Household Tasks 85
  C. Business, Finance, And Attractions 86
  D. Children And Pets 87

Part 9: Moving In   89
  A. Preparations 89
  B. If The Movers Unload 90
  C. If The Movers Unpack 94
  D. If You Unload And Unpack 95
  F. After You've Moved In 96

Part 10: International Moves   97
  A. Preparations 97
  B. Documentation 100
  C. Vehicles 102
  D. Organization 104
  E. Details, Details, Details 107
  F. Express Shipments 109
  G. Arriving 111

Part 11: After You Have Settled In   113
  A. Taking Care Of Business 113
  B. Children And Pets 115

Appendices
  A: The Floor Plan 117
  B: Househunting Checklist 121
  C: Making A Household Inventory 123
       Household Inventory Form 127
  D: Filing An Insurance Claim 129
  E: Your 'Last Box' 131
  F: Suggestions for Packing Your Car and Suitcase 133
  G: Items Which Movers Will Not Pack 137
  H: Other Helpful Sources 139

DEDICATION

To my husband, Keith
for his unfaltering love and support

To my children, Benjamin and Jonathan
who fill me with pride and joy

To my parents, Harold and Lois
for their unwavering love and generosity

INTRODUCTION

You have probably moved before. And you've probably vowed you would never do it again! But these are days of family mobility and fluctuating job markets. Such vows are idle threats. Moving has become a way of life.

This book will help make your next move easier and less stressful. It is a compilation of tested ideas that I assure you will save you many hours of frustration, reduce your anxiety, and make your next move a more pleasant experience. It will help you avoid the problems I learned to avoid the hard way—by trial and error—during more than twenty-five moves of my own.

What this book teaches you is organization. The more organized you are, the easier your move will be. Where moving is concerned, organization is at least two thirds of the battle. Good organization will spare you from the things that most people complain about: the endless little details, the minor things you either forget about or run out of time to do, the stress, the disorganization, the feeling that you are not in control.

Moving: A Complete Checklist and Guide for Relocation will help you plan and accomplish your next move, whether it is across town, across the country, or around the world. It is designed to be used, not just read. The checklists and timetables are presented in a logical order. Wide margins leave you plenty of room for your own notes and observations. The check-off format allows you to experience a sense of accomplishment as items are completed and the security of knowing you are not overlooking anything.

The keys to a successful move are planning ahead, doing a little each day, and scheduling at least one hour a day for yourself. Read, get some exercise, take a nap, or do whatever else helps alleviate the stress and fatigue you are undoubtedly feeling. Schedule one big task and several minor ones each day and you will be in good shape when moving day arrives.

The tips and recommendations are all based on my experiences. There is a reason for each one and a reason why each should be done at a particular time. Sometimes, the reason is as simple as this: it will save you time or effort when you move. At other times, the reason is much more concrete. For examples:

Why do I recommend buttoning the top buttons on dresses, shirts, coats, jackets, etc.? Because if you don't close these buttons, you will find your clothes in a wrinkled heap at the bottom of the wardrobe boxes when you unpack. You will have to rehang all of them, and you'll probably have to wash and iron more than a few of them, too.

Or, why do I recommend polishing your silver and putting it in air-tight plastic bags? Because it's easier to clean the silver *before* you move than it is to unpack and find all your silver tarnished and in need of polishing. If you polish it first and seal it in a bag, you won't have to deal with it while you are trying to get settled.

And why do I recommend washing out your trash cans? You'll find out when you start unpacking and discover that creative helpers or movers have left un-dumped garbage in the bottoms and packed lamp-shades and other household items on top.

Use this book to prepare for your next move. Dedicate more of your time to the important things like acclimating to your new surroundings, registering your children in school, getting the utilities hooked up, restocking the kitchen and refrigerator, and, of course, unpacking. Let everyone participate—even children can close up the top buttons, for example. A burden shared is lightly borne.

Using This Book

Become familiar with this book. Read it from cover to cover as soon as you know that you are going to be moving, or earlier if you can. Get an overview of what your move will involve at each stage of its process. Don't wait until the last minute to read a particular section. Being prepared is far preferable to being surprised.

Go through all of the checklists, even those which appear to be written for someone else. A few tips and suggestions appear in more than one place, but most are included in the section where they are considered most appropriate. Many of these will be useful for everyone who is moving, so take the time to look over each of the sections.

Look for icons in the margins. These are flags which will call your attention to items which may be useful for more than one type of move. A van icon alerts people who are moving themselves to a suggestion they might not otherwise have noticed. A moving-truck icon is a flag for those who are using professional movers. And an airliner icon marks an item which can make an international move easier.

Customize this book around your own needs. Every move is different. Yours may involve special considerations which could not be covered within the scope of this book. Use the wide margins and the open spaces to make notes and observations about your own special move.

Make this book a close friend. Use the lists. Check items off as you complete them. Write in the book. Highlight the tips you want to remember. Dog-ear the pages. Use paper clips, book marks, or sticky tabs to mark places.

Don't overlook the appendices. They include useful information which doesn't fit neatly into any single chapter. If you have ever tried to fit your furniture into a new home, you'll appreciate Appendix A, "The Floor Plan." If you should have to submit a claim to your insurance company, you'll be glad you read Appendix B, "Making A Household Inventory" and Appendix C, "Filing An Insurance Claim." Have you ever spent hours hunting through boxes, looking for something which you absolutely needed right away? You'll never do that again after you read Appendix D, "Your Last Box," and Appendix E, "Suggestions for Packing Your Car and Suitcase." Don't hire movers until you look over Appendix F, "Items Which Movers Will Not Pack." And if you want to dig more deeply into the subject of moving, look over Appendix G, "Other Helpful Sources."

Finally, keep this book at your side while you are moving. Put it in your suitcase or carry it in your car. Refer to it as often as you need. Don't just pack it and forget about it. You never know when you will need to refer to a checklist or to one of your notes.

Moving may never be a waltz through a rose garden. But it doesn't have to inspire vows of *never again!* If you follow the guidelines and suggestions in this book, you'll accomplish your move with a minimum of hassle and grief. With the stress of moving minimized, you can approach the transition as an opportunity to meet new friends, see a new part of the country or the world, and discover what you enjoy about your new home. Moving shouldn't get in the way of this exciting new adventure.

Have a great move! And write me in care of the publisher if you have any comments or suggestions for the next edition!

Planning Your Move

A: Preparation

- ☐ Write for information from the local Chamber of Commerce. Ask for a city map for house-hunting and future reference.

- ☐ Order a local newspaper subscription from your destination. This will give you insight into the housing market and help familiarize you with the area. Watch for realtor advertisements about "Relocating" and request their free literature.

- ☐ If you have children, discuss the upcoming move with them and invite them to participate in the planning. Encourage them to discuss their thoughts and feelings with you. Be positive. If the move is a happy experience for the children, they are more likely to adjust well. Your attitude is very influential. Your children will reflect it.

- ☐ Look at maps and globes with your children to show them where you're moving. Talk about the states or countries you will pass through during the move. Show them brochures from the Chamber of Commerce or tourist bureaus.

- ☐ Be sensitive to your family's concerns. Leaving friends and familiar surroundings behind and dealing with the unknown is difficult for everyone.

- ☐ If possible, arrange for the whole family to see the new location. This will eliminate some of the apprehension and reduce the stress and worry. If everyone is not able to go, take lots of pictures or

---

If You Are Selling Your House

• Put your home up for sale as soon as possible. Require that the settlement coincide with the date of your move.

• Do whatever touch up work is needed to make your property more appealing.

• Make sure your realtor is properly advertising the property and organizing open houses.

• Keep the house neat and clean inside and well groomed outside to give the appearance of what realtors call 'pride of ownership.'

• Make sure the entrance way creates a good first impression.

• When your house is being shown, turn on all the lights and open all the curtains and shades. This will give the rooms a bright and airy appearance and make the rooms look bigger.

• Always emphasize the good points of the house and neighborhood.

If you have time, you may prefer to put your house up *For Sale by Owner*. Create a handout with vital information. Place an advertisement in the local newspaper (in the classified and in the real estate sections) with an appealing picture, a description of the house, and your selling price. Selling your home without the services of a realtor can save you the six- or seven-percent realtor's commission. This can mean substantial savings.

---

videotape the neighborhood, schools, and points of interest.

☐ If you are able to choose the time of year when you move, consider the following advantages and disadvantages:

  • A summer move doesn't disrupt the school year and permits your child to complete the current grade with the same teacher and friends. On the other hand, if you move during the summer, you may arrive too late to sign your child up for organized summer activities unless you have done the paperwork before you move, sight unseen. You may also find that the children in your new neighborhood are away on vacation or at camp. Summer is also the peak season for movers, so it may be more difficult to get dates you desire.

- A move during the school year allows your child's new teachers to help with the transition to a new class. Your child will be able to meet other children more quickly and become involved immediately in various activities. Scheduling your move may be quite a bit easier, as well.

B: Budgeting

☐ Put a moving budget together by anticipating as many costs of your move as you can. Planning your trip well ahead of time and obtaining estimates promptly will help you identify all the costs.

☐ Develop a list of possible expenses and add to your list as new items become apparent. Your expenses will include both the obvious and the not-so-obvious, such as:

- Your house-hunting trip.
- The costs of buying a home.
- Moving expenses not covered by your employer.
- The costs of hiring professional movers.
- Do-it-yourself trailer rental.
- Transportation to your destination, including:
  - *Airline tickets;*
  - *Automobile expenses;*
  - *Restaurant meals and hotels.*
- Your first and last month's rent and/or damage deposits for an apartment or house rental.
- Utility deposits and fuel oil or wood for the fireplace in your new home.
- Final utility payments from your old home.
- Cost of the tow package if you decide to tow a vehicle.
- Car servicing.
- Kennel fees or costs to transport your pets.
- Professional house cleaners.
- Dry cleaning your rugs and drapes.
- New clothes and outer wear if you are moving to a different climate.
- New curtains, bathroom rug sets, shades, etc.
- Additional suitcases.

- Replacement paints, aerosols, cleaning supplies, groceries, etc.
- Credit reports sent to your new bank.
- Application and/or membership fees to clubs and organizations.
- Purging and certifying the propane tanks on your gas grill.
- Babysitters.
- Gifts for friends who help you pack and move.
- Lunch or doughnuts for helpers or movers on moving day.
- Stamps and change of address cards.
- Last-minute local sightseeing.

☐ Make your travel reservations early to qualify for discounts.

☐ If your company is paying your expenses, it will probably have a maximum weight allowance for your household goods. You will get a bill for the difference if you exceed the maximum weight. Budget for this—it is very expensive! Better yet, read Section 2B below and have a garage sale!

☐ If you are paying the movers, payment is normally due upon the delivery of your shipment and before unloading begins. Budget for this, allowing a little extra for unexpected costs, and be ready to have cash or a certified check available. (Some companies may also accept credit cards. Find out in advance.) If the balance due is more than your non-binding estimate (see page 18 below), you will have thirty days from delivery to pay the difference.

☐ If you are moving overseas, Part 10 includes a number of additional expenses for which you will need to budget.

C: A House-Hunting Trip

☐ Plan and budget for a house-hunting trip. Make your travel reservations as soon as possible to qualify for the best discounts.

☐ Get a realtor referral from someone you already know, or select a realtor from Better Business Bureau listings or the local newspaper. (Referrals are best, because they give you confidence that the realtor is credible and dependable.)

☐ Ask your real estate agent to send you relocation information about the local community. Ask for an area relocation guide. This can give you valuable information about the area, including an overview of the school systems in the area if you have children of school age.

☐ Make a list of your requirements and/or specifications for a house or apartment. Communicate this information to your realtor, along with an indication of your price range. Tell the agent when you will arrive on your house-hunting trip, and ask the realtor to line up several homes for you to visit after you arrive.

☐ Customize a copy of Appendix B, "House-Hunting Checklist," to suit your own needs. Fill in one copy of this checklist as a summary of your own requirements for a new home.

☐ Take several copies of the House-Hunting Checklist with you. Complete one for each home you look at, writing the street address on the top of each form. After you have looked at thirty or forty houses, these lists will come in very handy.

☐ Before you leave, measure your furniture, appliances, and rugs (see Appendix A, "The Floor

Plan," for more information). Take the dimensions of your larger items (king size beds or large living room or dining room sets, for example) with you so you can refer to all of them while house-hunting.

☐ Carry a notebook for notes and a camera for pictures so that you can remember what you saw. Bring a tape measure to ensure the rooms are big enough for you and all your furniture and appliances. Measure window sizes to determine if you will have to alter your drapes or buy new ones.

☐ Record room dimensions on your checklists or in your notebook. This will be crucial when you make your floor plan and experiment with room arrangements. See Appendix A, "The Floor Plan," for some useful tips.

☐ If you have children, consider the reputation of the school district and quality of the education before you are pick out a home. Make appointments to visit the schools in neighborhoods you are considering. Talk with principals and staff. If there is a local college at your destination, talk to recruiters and counselors about the local schools.

☐ Find out the enrollment requirements of each school so you will know the paperwork (medical records, health certificates, dental records, transcripts, etc.) and other prerequisites which you will need to provide before you can enroll your children.

☐ Research day-care and pre-school programs. Visit them and talk to parents and teachers so you can make an informed decision before placing your child in one.

☐ To judge an individual school or school system, consider the opportunities and advantages it can provide your children and its ability to fulfill your expectations as a parent.

☐ For guidelines on selecting a school, order a copy of the U.S. Department of Education's free brochure, "Choosing a School for Your Child." (See the bibliography for ordering information.)

☐ Evaluate the location and neighborhood of the homes you are considering. Find out about local facilities, shopping, hospital, transportation, and any other factors which are important to you and your family.

☐ Obtain a local public transportation map and schedule if you will need them.

☐ Make a list of what you will need upon arrival— dryer vent hoses, fences for pets, new carpeting, etc. Budget for these.

☐ If you plan to purchase your home, and especially if it is an older building, be sure to have it inspected by a professional inspection company or a structural engineer before you agree to the final purchase. Structural and other hidden problems can be expensive to correct and a real inconvenience to fix just when you are trying to get settled.

☐ Make notes about any repair work or painting that needs to be done to your new home. Allow enough time to complete these tasks *before* you move in. It's much more difficult to paint the walls or lay new carpet after your furniture has been delivered!

☐ Order a local phonebook. It will be invaluable for contacting schools, banks, utility companies, and other services and for getting information prior to your move.

☐ If it is appropriate, scout out the local job market ahead of time so you or a family member can set up some some job interviews during your house-hunting trip.

D: A Professional Move

□ Is your employer paying for your move? Get a copy of your company's relocation policy to determine if any restrictions and/or allowances will affect your move. For examples: Are there any weight limitations? Will the company help you sell your house or buy it from you if it doesn't sell? Will it pay for the professional movers and all your relocation expenses, and, if not, exactly what expenses will it cover?

□ Are you paying for the move out of your own pocket? Compare prices and services among several different moving companies. Get names of reputable and dependable movers from the Better Business Bureau and/or recommendations from friends. Be sure to choose companies approved by the Interstate Commerce Comission (ICC).

□ Have movers explain their estimates in detail. Discuss their rates, their liability for your household goods, their pickup and delivery, your claims protection, and anything else that might affect your move.

□ Find out if there will be any extra charges. Rates are normally based on the distance you are moving, the weight of your shipment, and the time of year (rates are higher in the summer). But you may be charged extra if there are more than a few front porch steps or a longer-than-normal distance from curbside to your house or elevator.

□ Ask for a separate estimate for your professional items, such as the professional books or job-related equipment which your employer might pay to move for you.

☐ Most prices quoted by movers are controlled by state tariffs (so much per pound or so much per carton). Be sure you discuss *how* they pack the cartons. For example, some movers may put only one lamp shade in a carton instead of nesting several together. Practices like this can push your moving cost well above the estimate because of the additional number of cartons used.

☐ Review Section 1F, "Packing Tips." Even though you are using professional movers and packers, you will still need to pack the items you are personally carrying with you. You may also be able to save money by packing some of your other things yourself. (Be advised, however: few movers will accept liability for damage to items they did not pack.)

☐ Find out if the organizations to which you belong (auto clubs, senior citizen associations, etc.) have arranged for discounts from selected movers.

☐ Once you have chosen a company, decide whether you want a *binding* or a *non-binding* estimate.

• A binding estimate specifies the exact cost of the move, including all services requested and/or needed at the time the estimate is made. A binding estimate is guaranteed to be a final cost, but it does not include additional services requested later. Nor will a binding estimate be adjusted if you sell some heavy furniture or appliances after the estimate has been accepted. Make sure all of your possessions are included in the estimate. Movers do not have to move any items that were not in the original, binding estimate.

• A non-binding estimate is not final. It is more flexible, however. The total cost of your move will be demened by the standard factors of weight, distance, materials, labor, and services applied at the time of the move to your actual shipment.

☐ Contact movers as soon as possible ahead of time (eight or more weeks if possible) in order to schedule your move during the dates you request.

☐ Plan your packing and loading dates carefully, and avoid putting your goods in temporary storage if you can. Not only is the cost of unloading and reloading your goods into storage expensive, but the more your possessions are handled, the greater the possibility of damage.

☐ When you contact the movers, have the following information ready:

- Your desired packing and loading dates. Be flexible and realistic. If your shipment is large, for example, the movers may need more than one day to pack your household goods.
- The date you will arrive at your destination and the date when the movers will be able to deliver your household goods.
- The type of shipments you anticipate—regular household goods shipment, storage shipment, partial shipment to a different address, express overseas shipment, etc.
- A list of large or unusual items (pianos, pool tables, wall units, king size beds, grandfather clocks, china cabinets, etc.) which will require special packing materials.

☐ Schedule an appointment for a moving company representative to come to your home for a pre inspection. Ask the agent how much time the movers will need to pack and load your household goods and how long your shipment will take to arrive at its destination.

☐ To get an accurate cost estimate, show movers *everything*. Don't forget the attic, garage, basement, or closets. The weight of your shipment, the distance moved, and the cost of packing materials and labor all will affect the estimate. On a local move, the cost is generally based on an hourly rate and the total time needed to move your goods.

☐ At the pre-inspection, specify that you will want mirror cartons, mattress cartons, or other packaging for your special items. Express your desire for clean vans and, if appropriate, high quality crates.

☐ Tell the moving company about any special requirements which might affect the shipment (your requirements or those of the country of destination, if you are moving overseas).

☐ Ask how many packers will work on the job—the fewer there are, the more days it will take to pack. This will help you plan your moving schedule more accurately.

☐ Movers will not routinely disconnect appliances, VCRs, antennas, or other equipment. If you request it ahead of time, the moving company can arrange for appliances to be serviced (prepared for the move). The fee for servicing is usually added to the Bill of Lading, which describes your shipment and the terms and conditions which apply.

☐ If you have items going into storage or if you are requesting other types of shipments, plan to have these goods picked up *before* your household goods are loaded.

☐ Keep the moving company and other offices informed of any changes to your moving dates, contact phone numbers, or any other important information.

☐ Review the next section, "A Do-It-Yourself Move," for additional tips and pointers. Depending on your furniture and the distance you are moving, a do-it-yourself move might be more economical.

E: A Do-It-Yourself Move

☐ Determine if a do-it-yourself move would be appropriate. (A do-it-yourself move is worth considering when you are making a short move across town, when you are moving relatively small amounts of goods, when your move is not underwritten by an employer, or whenever financial considerations make it necessary.)

☐ Decide if you are prepared to do everything associated with the move, from packing to truck rental to loading and unloading.

☐ Start collecting clean boxes, unprinted newsprint paper, and other packing material as soon as you know you will be moving. You may be able to purchase unprinted newsprint from a local newspaper, paper warehouse, or art-supply store. Don't use *printed* newsprint...it stains.

☐ Get heavy-duty cartons from liquor stores, supermarkets, and other stores. You can also buy movers' cartons from paper warehouses and from mail order supply houses (if you plan far enough in advance).

☐ Get a supply of bubble wrap for packing fragile items.

☐ Review Section 1F, "Packing Tips."

☐ Visit your local trailer rental dealers and franchises. Ask questions! Trailer dealers have specific answers about such things as choosing the correct truck or trailer; renting accessories; calculating box requirements; packing particular items of property; loading trailers properly; and reserving storage space at your destination. Many also have racks of useful and free or low-cost literature.

☐ Compare the prices and options available—one-way rental rates, bumper hitches, hand trucks, side-view mirrors, furniture pads, boxes and packing material, tape, etc.

☐ Three to four weeks in advance of your move, reserve a truck or trailer and any other items you will need from the trailer rental company.

☐ Consider getting liability insurance for the rental truck or trailer. These can be expensive to fix or replace if you have an accident.

☐ Ask friends in advance to help load and unload your trailer. You will be surprised at how quickly the move goes with five or six helpers.

☐ When moving day comes, make a party out of it. Offer sandwiches or pizza and soft drinks. Beer is a nice addition, too, but only *after* the job is done.

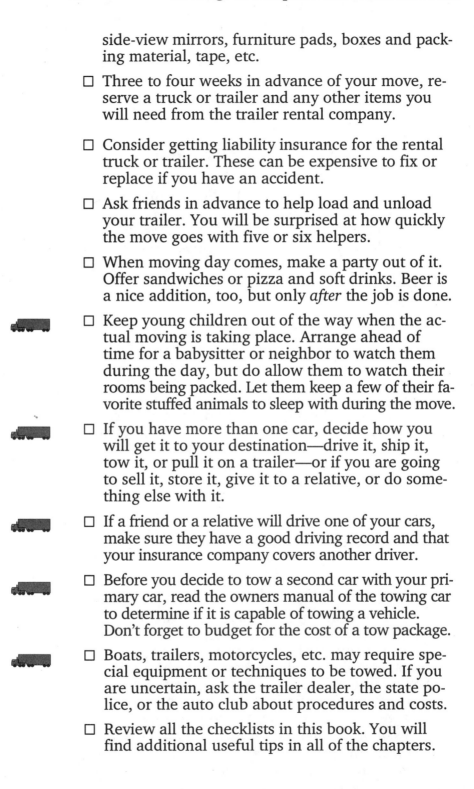

☐ Keep young children out of the way when the actual moving is taking place. Arrange ahead of time for a babysitter or neighbor to watch them during the day, but do allow them to watch their rooms being packed. Let them keep a few of their favorite stuffed animals to sleep with during the move.

☐ If you have more than one car, decide how you will get it to your destination—drive it, ship it, tow it, or pull it on a trailer—or if you are going to sell it, store it, give it to a relative, or do something else with it.

☐ If a friend or a relative will drive one of your cars, make sure they have a good driving record and that your insurance company covers another driver.

☐ Before you decide to tow a second car with your primary car, read the owners manual of the towing car to determine if it is capable of towing a vehicle. Don't forget to budget for the cost of a tow package.

☐ Boats, trailers, motorcycles, etc. may require special equipment or techniques to be towed. If you are uncertain, ask the trailer dealer, the state police, or the auto club about procedures and costs.

☐ Review all the checklists in this book. You will find additional useful tips in all of the chapters.

F: Packing Tips

- ☐ Get a supply of packing boxes from a moving or trailer-renting company. Most will refund the full purchase price of any boxes you do not use.

- ☐ Pack a little each day, starting with the items you won't need until after you have moved.

- ☐ Pack room by room, keeping similar items together. Clearly mark the boxes with a detailed description of contents. Where appropriate, label boxes with the word *Fragile*. If you know it, also indicate the room in which the contents should be placed when you are moving in.

- ☐ If you will not be moving directly into your new home, don't pack any foods which could spoil.

- ☐ Pack boxes firmly to prevent the contents from shifting during your move. Use crumpled paper for padding. Seal boxes tightly with wide packing tape.

- ☐ Use appropriate-sized boxes. Those which are too heavy can hurt your back, while those which are packed too loosely can be crushed in transit.

- ☐ Pack books and heavy items in smaller boxes. Use large boxes for lighter items.

- ☐ Pack phonograph records and CDs vertically in boxes. Don't stack them flat.

- ☐ Place heavier items in the bottom of the box and lighter items on top.

- ☐ Separate items with paper to prevent scratches caused by rubbing.

- ☐ While packing or unpacking breakables, hold them over a box. They will be less likely to break if you drop them.

- ☐ Remove lids from jars and ceramics and wrap them separately.

- ☐ To avoid spills and leakage, seal any opened boxes and bottles before you pack them.

- ☐ Pack cleaning supplies and poisons in separate boxes from your other household goods.

- ☐ Take the lampshades off your lamps and pack them separately. Shades can be nested one inside another with a layer of paper between each.

- ☐ Protect breakables and pictures by wrapping them separately and placing them between blankets, pillows, kitchen or bathroom towels. You can also wrap them in bubble wrap.

- ☐ Use mirror cartons for your pictures and mirrors.

- ☐ Pad the hooks on the backs of picture, paintings, and mirrors with extra paper before you wrap the entire piece.

- ☐ Carefully wrap individual pieces of glassware in clean, unprinted newsprint so you won't have to wash them when you unpack. Put extra paper inside of glasses and cups.

- ☐ Fill clothes hampers, baskets, and any other clean containers with blankets, linens, towels, etc.

- ☐ Purchase wardrobe boxes for your hanging clothes. These may seem expensive, but they allow you to pack clothes directly from the closet and to hang them up immediately upon arrival with a minimum of effort.

- ☐ Fold clean drapes over wooden hangers and hang them in a wardrobe box so you won't have to iron them at your destination.

- ☐ Save your wardrobe boxes. After you are settled, you can use them for storing out-of-season clothes and jackets.

- ☐ Remove the glass shelves from cabinets and pack them separately.

Some Important Pointers For Lifting

• Always bend your knees and lift or lower items with your leg muscles, not your back. Keep your back straight.

• Keep your feet apart for balance when you are lifting.

• Carry items close to your body.

• Keep walkways, stairs, and paths free of obstacles.

• Never carry an item if it blocks your vision.

• Ask for help if an item is too heavy for you to lift safety.

• Use dollies and furniture straps for moving large or heavy items. Ask for proper instructions when you rent or buy them.

• *Use Common Sense!* Don't rush. Don't show off. Do it safely.

☐ Secure cabinets and cabinet doors with string or rubber bands to prevent them from swinging open during your move.

☐ Dismantle large furniture items such as beds, china cabinets, kitchen and dining room tables, or grandfather clocks before moving.

☐ Remove castors from couches, dressers, and other furniture and place them inside bureau drawers.

☐ Wrap heavy, breakable, or easily-lost parts separately, and label the container with the contents.

☐ Steam-clean your rugs or have them professionally cleaned. When they are dry, roll them up with their corresponding pads and secure them with tape. Use a magic marker to write the dimensions on the underside of the rugs (write on masking tape if there is a danger the ink may bleed through) and the room in which they should be placed.

☐ Pack rugs last so they can be the first items unloaded at your destination. Roll them out in their new locations before you place any furniture or boxes in your new home.

☐ If you are moving a washing machine, secure the agitator with a styrofoam washer block (available from a moving company).

☐ Follow the instructions in Section 6B for moving appliances and electronic equipment.

☐ If you are going to transport flammable or explosive items, check first with the state police. State and federal agencies may have issued guidelines or regulations which you will need to follow.

☐ When it is time to start loading, make sure that children and pets stay out of the way.

☐ If you have rented a trailer, take care to distribute the weight of your shipment properly within the trailer and not to exceed the trailer's weight capacity. Excess and/or improperly distributed weight is dangerous!

☐ When loading a trailer and again when unloading it, place your boxes so that you can read the contents written on the box.

☐ No matter how well you pack the trailer, contents are likely to shift during your move. Protect furniture and appliance surfaces by using proper padding.

☐ Make sure you have proper locks for your trailer, and keep the trailer locked at all times.

G: Insurance

☐ Inventory your household goods while you are preparing for your move (See Appendix C). This inventory will help you identify where your insurance coverage needs to be updated.

☐ Discuss your move with your household goods insurance company to determine if your household goods/personal property coverage is adequate. Make sure you have sufficient coverage for your property, your car, and your high-value items.

☐ Consult your insurance agent. Make sure you have sufficient coverage for your liability during the move as well as your property.

☐ The moving company and your insurance company can give you valuable advice on basic valuation coverage, full replacement protection, and other insurance questions. As of this writing, the standard coverage from most movers is around sixty cents per pound of shipment. If your household insurance company covers household goods in full during transportation, you will not need to buy insurance from the moving company.

☐ Check the status of your household goods insurance for your new home. Some policies remain unchanged when you move, requiring only a change-of-address. Others may require a recalculation of your premium to the prevailing rates at your new location.

☐ If friends will be helping you move, consider taking out a liability insurance policy. You can't be too cautious where injuries may occur.

☐ Evaluate the current coverage of your life, health, dental and other insurance policies as well.

H: Business, Finance, And Attractions

☐ Advise your landlord, realtor, or housing office as soon as you know when you will be moving out.

☐ Contact your attorney and resolve any unfinished legal matters.

☐ Verify that your wills are up to date. If they are being drawn up, make sure they will be finished prior to your move.

☐ Contact city and county assessors to make sure all your taxes have been paid.

☐ Pay any outstanding parking tickets.

☐ If you will need to transfer a professional license to a new state, start the process as soon as you know your moving dates.

☐ Get a driver's manual from your destination state and begin brushing up on the new state laws.

☐ Plan to mail or hand-carry your important records (including school records and college transcripts) to your new destination. Hand-carrying is more reliable, because you don't have to depend on others to get your records delivered.

☐ Make sure you have all current and complete addresses of your doctors, dentist, X-ray labs, lawyer, stockbroker, banker, veterinarian, pharmacist, and other professionals in case you need to contact them after the move. Not all doctors, for example, will let you hand-carry your records. Many will release your records only to another professional upon written request. Similarly, X-rays are usually not included in your records and must be specifically requested by your new doctor or dentist directly. (Most X-ray labs will charge you five dollars or so for each copy you request).

☐ Plan local trips to see the attractions in your area that you haven't visited yet or to visit your favorite ones again.

☐ Start using up your coupons (movie theater passes, free passes, discounts, green stamps, etc.).

I: Address Labels

☐ Make a list of your friends, business accounts, professional services, insurance agencies, banks and credit unions, charge cards, record and book clubs, catalog companies, investment companies, churches, lawyers, doctors and dentists, unions, stockbroker, utility companies, magazines, clubs organizations and associations, alumni associations, motor vehicle bureau, voter registration, state and federal tax bureaus, Social Security, Veterans Administration, present and future post offices, and anyone else who needs to be notified that you are moving. List account numbers also, if applicable.

☐ Get a stack of change-of-address cards from the post office. Begin notifying each person on your list. Doctors and dentists can be notified in person. Utility companies can be advised by phone. Almost everyone else should receive a change of address card. Sending a few cards each day will make the task less burdensome.

☐ One way to simplify and expedite this procedure is to keep a list of all your accounts and friends on your computer and print them out on mailing labels. For each change-of-address card, print out one set of mailing labels with your old address and another set with your new address. Then attach a label to the appropriate box on each change-of-address card. This method can save you an enormous amount of time.

☐ If it is close to the end of the year, you can send out your holiday greeting cards early instead of change of address cards. This will save a lot of time and postage.

☐ As soon as you know your new phone number, you can add it to some or all of your change-of-address cards.

☐ Start saving all address labels from the magazines and catalogs you subscribe to for your change of address cards.

☐ Two or three months before your move (or as soon as you know your new address) start notifying magazine publishers of your change of address. It speeds up the process if you use the mailing labels you have been saving when you notify the magazines.

☐ Military personnel on PCS moves can write *Official Orders* on the Postmaster's Change of Address card to ensure magazines and all correspondence will be forwarded postage free. (It is no longer necessary to attach a copy of your orders.)

☐ Make a list of those businesses which you can contact by phone or toll-free number. Some will accept a change of address verbally, which saves a lot of time and postage.

J: Moving With A Pet

☐ If you are driving, plan your route to visit friends along the way or to stay at campgrounds or hotels that accept pets.

☐ Never leave your pet in a closed or locked car. Winter and summer temperatures become extreme very quickly.

☐ If you will be traveling long distances by car, consider buying a ventilated pet carrier.

☐ If you are flying, arrange for your pet's transportation when you make your own reservations. The cost of transporting your pet will be substantially less if your pet travels on the same flight as you.

☐ Request a direct flight if one exists or the shortest route with the fewest stops otherwise. Try to avoid plane changes and long layovers.

☐ Ask the airline about its procedures for transporting animals, its requirements for veterinary certificates, its check-in and advanced boarding regulations, and any options it may offer for transporting your pet.

☐ If you have to send your pet ahead of you, make arrangements for airport transfers and delays and for picking up your pet at your destination.

☐ Your pet will probably need to be crated in flight. Build your own crate according to airline specifications, or purchase wooden or metal crates from the airline. Wooden crates might require additional holes bored on the sides to increase ventilation.

☐ Don't get a crate that is too big for the animal. If you do, your pet can be thrown around during take off and landing.

☐ Arrange for crating well in advance of departure to allow plenty of time for your pet to get used to its crate or container. This will help reduce your pet's stress during travel.

☐ Enclose your pet's health certificate and proof of vaccination in a sealed plastic bag. In another sealed plastic bag, attach a leash, enough food for the entire trip, and bowls. Fasten these bags securely to the outside of your pet's crate.

☐ Make sure the crate is clearly labeled with your new address, phone number, flight itinerary, and destination. Get a *Live Animal* sticker from the airline and attach it prominently to the crate.

☐ Collect veterinarian records and obtain a health certificate indicating that all shots are up to date. In most states, a rabies shot is required for licensing. Veterinarians, the humane society, and kennels can provide information on various state requirements. (If you are taking your pet overseas, see the additional notes in Part 10.)

☐ Ask your veterinarian about medications for your pet while traveling. If you will be flying, ask about sedatives for your pet.

☐ When you deliver your pet to the airport, make sure the pilot of the airplane is informed that an animal will be on board so that the cargo hold can be pressurized. Ask that cargo handlers give water to the animal.

☐ Have a identification tag made up for your pet with your new address and phone number. If you don't know your address yet, put the address and phone number of a friend or relative who can be contacted.

☐ Make sure your pet wears a collar with a current rabies tag and current identification. Feed it six hours before traveling and give it water two hours before. Exercise it before loading.

☐ Put a blanket and one of your pet's favorite toys in the crate.

☐ If you are unable to take your pet with you, find it
a good home, preferably with a relative or friend.

Six To Eight Weeks Before You Move

A: Sorting Through Your Belongings

☐ Go through each room and every closet, cabinet, shelf, and drawer. Decide what you are going to move, what you are going to discard, and what you are going to sell or donate. Set a goal to do one room each day until you are finished.

☐ Start weeding out the unneeded, unwanted, and unused items in your house, garage, basement, attic, patio, car, and elsewhere. Remember, the more you move, the heavier your property is, and the more your household goods weigh, the more your move will cost.

☐ Sort through childrens' rooms for games, toys, and clothes they are no longer using. If your children are old enough, let them participate by going through their own rooms and deciding what they don't want to keep. Separate their discards into trash, yard sale, give away, and donate piles.

☐ Clean out your file cabinets. Discard all the files and papers which you no longer need.

☐ Get rid of old magazines and duplicate catalogs.

☐ Throw out all unlabeled and outdated medicines in your medicine cabinets and bathroom closets.

☐ Discard your unwanted perfumes, aftershaves, colognes, fingernail polishes, and other cosmetics.

B: Holding A Garage Sale

☐ Hold a garage sale. This can be a big money maker! Don't throw anything away unless it is unrepairable. Even the 'freebees' and 'junk' that kids collect can be sold for a penny or two each. Kids gobble these up, and your children can make a little money by themselves to boot.

☐ Label everything with a price ahead of time. Be realistic in your pricing—what would *you* be willing to pay for this item? Even then, be prepared to haggle.

☐ Give yourself several days for sorting and labeling items. This is a surprisingly time-consuming activity.

☐ Place an ad in the newspaper. Put signs up in the neighborhood to advertise your sale. Make your signs large enough to be read easily, and use a prominent attention-getting headline.

☐ If you are selling large or expensive items, take out a special ad in the paper calling attention to them.

☐ Arrange for a baby sitter to keep an eye on any young children during your garage sale.

☐ Display your garage-sale merchandise on tables and/or blankets.

☐ Set up your displays the night before in your garage. Otherwise get up early on the morning of the sale to set up properly and prepare yourself for the sale.

☐ Be ready for the early birds who want to scoop up the bargains.

☐ Arrange your items neatly and attractively. Make sure everything is clean.

☐ Wear a 'fanny pack' around your waist to hold your money. Start with lots of change and only accept checks from people you know.

☐ Anything not sold can be donated to charities or given to friends and relatives. Books will normally be accepted at the local library. Request a receipt so you can claim the deduction on your income tax return.

☐ Remove your signs after the sale is over!

C: Making an Inventory and a List of Shipments

☐ Make an inventory of all your household items and the contents of your home. (If you have an inventory from a previous move, you can use it after you have updated it.)

☐ Appendix C outlines the basics of making a household inventory and includes a sample inventory form. Follow its suggestions to design your own form. Or, you can get prepared inventory forms from your household goods insurance company or any of the professional moving companies. You can also obtain relatively inexpensive home-inventory software for your home computer.

☐ If you discover an item missing after your move, it will have been itemized on your inventory. Even if you are making a do-it-yourself move, the inventory will help you verify that everything has arrived safely.

☐ Photograph or video tape your valuables—jewelry, antiques, coins, silver, collectables, guns, artwork, musical instruments, etc. This makes dealing with your insurance company much easier if you should have an accident or a loss.

☐ Have your high-value items appraised.

☐ Keep a record of the make and model of all your appliances, including radios, TV's, computers, and other home-electronic items. Record all serial numbers.

☐ Keep your inventory up to date. Store it in a safe place to prevent loss or damage.

☐ Keep a separate inventory of your professional items (reference books, papers, instruments, tools and equipment, specialized clothing, etc.). This will help you organize your professional items into one room when your goods are delivered.

☐ Make separate lists for each of the following items:

- The household goods you are taking with you.
- The items you plan to store.
- Professional items.
- Items for your 'last box.' These are the items you will be unpacking first (See Appendix E, "Your 'Last Box').
- Items for your suitcases, such as clothes for a different climate (see Appendix F, "Suggestions for Packing Your Car and Suitcase").
- Valuables you will keep in your possession during your move (also see Appendix F).
- Flammables, aerosols, and other items which you or the movers cannot or will not move (see Appendix G, "Items Which Movers Will Not Pack").

☐ If you are moving overseas (see Chapter 10), make additional lists for:

- Items to be sent by express shipment.
- Items to be sent by unaccompanied baggage shipment.
- Items which have to be inspected or quarantined (See Section 10D, below).

D: Considering Storage

☐ Do you have property which you want to keep but which you are unwilling or unable to take with you? Consider storing it. For example, if you are moving to a smaller home but don't want to sell furniture which will not fit, you can put it it in storage. Large tools and work benches can be stored if there is no workspace in your new home. Air conditioners and other appliances which are incompatible with your new home as well as clothes which are inappropriate for your new climate can also be put away for your return.

☐ Inspect the storage facility carefully. Ask such questions as: Is it clean? Are there palates for raising stored items off the floor? Are the rugs rolled or folded and is the rolling or folding done by you or the facility? Are rugs also stored off the floor? Is there evidence of any water damage? Are there sprinklers, fire alarms, and security devices?

☐ Find out if insurance is available through the storage facility or if you will need to get it from your insurance agent.

☐ Clean your property and make any necessary repairs before you store it.

E: Household Tasks

☐ If you are a renter, ask your landlord or housing office for a checklist of the items which will be inspected when you leave.

☐ Decide if you will have the house professionally cleaned or if you will clean it yourself. Arrange for the cleaners and budget for this (prices vary, so get a few bids). If you are cleaning it yourself, plan to leave enough time after your household goods have been removed and before you leave the area.

☐ If you live in a high-rise apartment, reserve the service elevator on your moving day.

☐ If you are married and especially if your spouse will not be home during the move, the two of you should make a lists of things that you each prefer to do without help. For example, who is responsible for unhooking the stereo or the computer? Who handles the tools or the kitchen appliances? Who packs the camera equipment?

☐ Start fixing the little things that need to be fixed. Don't wait until the last minute.

☐ Finish any sewing or mending which you've been putting off.

☐ Don't forget to spend an hour a day on yourself.

F: Business, Finance, And Attractions

☐ Establish credit in your new home town. Your bank or credit union can probably recommend a counterpart. Ask for a letter of introduction along with a credit rating, both of which will minimize processing delays after you move in.

☐ Talk to your banker about transferring funds to another bank. Establish an account in your new location before you move. (You can open accounts by mail if necessary).

☐ Using out-of-state checks can sometimes be difficult, so order new checks as soon as your address is established.

☐ If you are unable to open an account in advance of your arrival, arrange to have sufficient cash or travelers' checks to cover the expenses you will incur before you can open an account.

☐ At the appropriate time after your new account is established, transfer any allotments or automatic deposits or withdrawals to your new bank or cancel them entirely.

☐ Decide how and when to close out your local bank accounts.

☐ Ask your church, schools, doctors, dentists, and other individuals or organizations to recommend contacts in your new area.

☐ Apply now for new memberships at clubs, day-care centers, and other organizations, especially if there are waiting lists.

☐ Arrange to sell any equity you have in your country club, yacht club, etc. Transfer any memberships in service clubs such as Rotary, Masonic Lodge, Kiwanis, or Lions.

☐ Make sure you have a list of your credit cards, along with account numbers, addresses, and phone numbers, in case of theft during your move.

☐ Start closing your local charge accounts (drug stores, department stores, etc). Retain major credit cards until you can get new ones issued from your new location (Visa or MasterCard, oil company cards, national retail chains, for example).

☐ Obtain an IRS Moving Expense form from the library, Post Office, or Internal Revenue Service. This will be easier to fill out now than it will be next year.

Four and Five Weeks before You Move

3

A: Starting To Clean

☐ Start cleaning your furniture and household goods a little each day. Your furniture will look nice when it is unloaded, and you won't have to worry about cleaning it as soon as you move in. You can use the extra time to get settled.

☐ While you are cleaning, check the condition of your furniture. If your furniture will be moved by professionals, this allows you to make sure that the movers accurately note existing furniture damage on their inventory sheets.

☐ Use colored wax crayons from the hardware store to cover any furniture scratches. This makes it easier to identify new scratches caused during your move. If the damage was caused by movers, this will also make it easier to file and document a damage claim.

☐ During your cleaning and organizing, keep a running list of items you'll need to replace when you relocate. This saves repeated trips to the store while you're getting settled. Be sure you have included these replacement costs in your budget.

☐ Clean the couch upholstery and put on a protectant such as Scotchguard®.

☐ Wax your wood furniture.

☐ Polish your silver, copper, and brass items and seal them in airtight bags.

☐ If you are doing it yourself, begin washing your crystal glasses and fine china and packing them as soon as it is practical. See Section 1F for packing tips.

☐ Clean out your junk drawers.

☐ Wash the fireplace tools and clean out the chimney.

☐ Drain the oil from oil lamps and allow the wicks to dry.

☐ Wash your doilies and store them in the linen closet.

☐ Wash all stuffed animals.

☐ If you are using movers, take any remaining stickers from a previous move off of your furniture. This will eliminate the confusion of duplicate numbers when the movers take inventory. (This is a good job for children. Pay them a little something—say, a penny for each sticker they find.)

B: Taking A Food Inventory

☐ Inventory the food in your cupboards, refrigerator, and freezer. Place a list of the contents of your freezer on the freezer door. Frozen items will have to be given away or discarded when you move, so plan your meals to use up as much frozen food as you can. Cross off each item as you use it.

☐ Between now and your move, buy perishables only as you need them.

☐ Also plan your meals to use up canned goods and boxed foods. If you plan well, you will be left with only a small amount of food to give away. You can save a lot of money by planning ahead and using what you have in stock.

C: Household Tasks

☐ If you will not need them in your new home, sell your blinds, drapes, and carpets. If you know who will be moving into your current home, offer these to them first.

☐ Stain, paint, and touch up any household items that need it. This will save you from having to do these chores after you move. If you are being moved professionally, this will also minimize the *existing damage* notations the movers will make on inventory sheets.

☐ Reseed the yard and trim shrubs, if necessary. Leaving the property looking neat and cared for is a nice touch, regardless of whether you are selling or giving up a rental.

☐ Remember to give yourself at least an hour a day.

D: Business, Finance, And Attractions

- ☐ Make medical and dental appointments if they are due. Ask your doctor and dentist to recommend professionals in your new location.

- ☐ Schedule physical examinations for your children if they are required by the new school.

- ☐ Have prescriptions written and filled. Get copies of your prescriptions if your doctor will write them for you. If you are moving overseas or to an area where it is not added to the tap water, you may also want to get a prescription for dental fluoride. Keep all prescription medicines in their original containers while you are traveling.

- ☐ Start dry-cleaning your clothes. Don't pack them dirty, especially if you are moving to an area where the climate or the seasons are different.

- ☐ If this is a do-it-yourself move, reserve your truck or trailer. Get packing cartons from the rental agency. (See Section 1E).

- ☐ Start updating your resume.

- ☐ Give advance resignation notice for your job, if applicable.

- ☐ Ask your employer and supervisor for letters of recommendation and letters of introduction. Obtain W-2 forms if possible. (If not, verify that your employer has your correct forwarding address).

- ☐ Get letters of introduction from your church, business associates, and any clubs or organizations to which you belong.

Two and Three Weeks before You Move

4

A: Preparations

☐ If you will be arriving at your destination before your household goods, make arrangements to stay with acquaintances or make reservations at a local hotel or motel for the period until your shipment gets there.

☐ Confirm all your other travel arrangements and reservations.

☐ If you will be traveling by car:

- have the vehicle serviced. Change the oil and oil filter, the points, and the plugs. Get the car lubed, repair any trouble spots, and check the tires, brakes, fluids, clutch, transmission, radiator, alternator, battery, etc.
- Buy a supply of radiator hoses, windshield wipers, belts, oil and antifreeze, flares, and those spare parts which may be hard to find, especially if you are going overseas.
- Be sure you have a jack and a small tool box for emergencies in the car.
- Order a trip itinerary and maps from an auto club or travel service if you haven't already done so.

☐ If you will be using movers and will be unable to be at home on moving day, arrange for someone to act as your representative. Notify the moving company.

☐ Consider staying in a hotel room or with friends the night your household goods are loaded. Make any necessary reservations or preparations.

☐ Make special arrangements for children and pets. Both should be out of the way on moving day.

☐ Make a special point of giving yourself some time. Things are starting to get hectic, but it is important not to ignore your personal well-being.

B: Household Tasks

☐ Remove any window air conditioners. Clean them and change the filters.

☐ Finish minor repairs and projects around the home. Don't leave these things undone.

☐ Wash your bathroom rug sets.

☐ Return library books, video tapes, neighbors' and friends' tools, etc.

☐ Label loose keys and put them on a key chain.

☐ Tape miscellaneous or loose parts to the item they fit. Otherwise, label and store them in ziploc bags to make them easy to find and retrieve later. Put these bags in your 'last box' so they are readily available on move-in day.

☐ Eat and drink up! The more food you have to give away, the more it is going to cost you.

C: Business, Finance, And Attractions

☐ Notify all utilities (telephone, gas, electric, water, cable) of your exact shut-off date. Ask for pro-rated bills for the last month and refunds of any deposits. Tell your fuel oil, water, and electric companies the date when they should take their final readings.

☐ Plan to keep your phone, water, and electricity hooked up until you have moved out and the place is clean.

☐ Contact the utility companies at your destination. Find out if you'll need to make any deposits and tell them the day on which you want service started. Arrange for fuel delivery, if necessary. (These costs should already be budgeted.)

☐ If you have not already done so, obtain your new telephone number from the business office of your new phone company. Where appropriate, put it on your change-of-address cards. Instruct the telephone company to give out your new phone number upon request.

☐ Let the newspaper, gardener, diaper service, garbage collection, cleaners, and other services know the date on which they should discontinue service.

☐ If you will need an appliance serviceman to prepare/disconnect your computer, VCR, television, or other appliances, make arrangements now for service on the day before your move. Call around for the best prices.

☐ If you are disconnecting gas appliances, a gas company representative should disconnect the gas lines and cap the pipes.

☐ Make any necessary arrangements to have your appliances reconnected at your destination.

☐ Arrange to have your grandfather clock, pool table, or other large items disassembled by an expert, if necessary. Contact the store where you purchased the items if the store is local.

☐ Make sure that anyone who owes you a refund— your landlord, utility companies, clubs, etc.—has your new address. If you can, get your refunds before you leave. It will save you correspondence and phone calls later.

D: Garage, Patio And Outdoor Equipment

☐ Inspect your outside items for gypsy moths. If an infestation is found, have it treated. (This is a federal requirement).

☐ Sort through your garage, porch, patio, and yard items, including those in drawers and on shelves. Set aside everything, such as flammables, paints, and aerosals, which movers will not pack or transport (see Appendix G) or which you do not want to carry. Check with your local waste management office. Some of these items may be considered hazardous waste and require special disposal.

☐ Hose down and scrub your outdoor items (golf clubs, ladders, patio furniture, recreational and camping items, building materials, yard and garden items, outdoor play equipment, car equipment, etc.). Let children hose down and wash their bikes, scooters, and other toys and paraphernalia.

☐ Remove peg board and hooks in the patio and garage if you are taking them with you.

☐ Clean your barbeque grill and pack the removable parts. Have propane gas tanks purged and certified. (Movers will not pack uncertified tanks. However, this is a good idea even if you are moving yourself.)

☐ Clean your camping porta-potti if you have one.

☐ Clean patio, driveway, and garage floor stains. (Cover fresh-oil stains with sawdust or kitty litter for several days. These will soak up the oil and remove the stain.)

- ☐ Take down any outdoor utility sheds or play equipment which you are not leaving behind.

- ☐ Get any items you will be taking with you out of storage. Clean these items at this time.

- ☐ Decide if you will want (or need) to hold a second garage sale.

- ☐ Sell or give away firewood and scrap lumber.

E: Food, Plants, Liquor

☐ Cook some meals ahead of time and freeze them for use during the days immediately before your move. Grill them (before you clean your grill) to use up propane, charcoal, or lighter fluid).

☐ Decide what to do with your houseplants. Movers can refuse to transport these, and some states prohibit the importation of plants from another state. Contact the agriculture department of your destination state to find out if you can bring your plants with you.

☐ Be prepared to sell houseplants or to give them away. Even if you are able to take your plants with you, consider how well they would survive the trip in your car or in a moving van without sun or water for days or even weeks.

☐ If you decide to transport the plants yourself, don't plan to put them in the trunk or expose them to extreme temperature changes. You'll need to secure the pots so they can't move and to prevent the leaves from resting against windows, where they can be burned by the sun.

☐ Plan a neighborhood farewell party to drink up your open bottles of liquor. You can pack open bottles in your own trunk, trailer, or van (not in passenger areas, however), but movers will not transport any open bottles.

☐ Clean the inside of your cookie jar.

☐ Clean the microwave, can opener, and other small appliances in your kitchen.

F: Friends And Acquaintances

☐ If you have children, take pictures of their friends and start a scrapbook. Collect addresses and phone numbers so your kids can keep in touch at holidays and other times.

☐ Have your friends pick up any items you are giving away. These should all be out of the way before you begin packing in earnest.

☐ Collect any items which you have loaned to neighbors or friends. Return those which you have borrowed. Pick up items on lay away, anything being repaired or dry cleaned, film being developed, and any other similar articles.

☐ Donate other things to charity. Get a receipt for tax purposes.

☐ Start saying farewell to friends and neighbors. Making just a few calls a day will give you more time as moving day approaches for last minute things.

☐ Give your new address and phone number in writing to your friends when you see them.

☐ Continue using up your coupons (movie theaters, free passes, green stamps, pool passes, etc). Give the rest away.

One Week Before You Move

A: Cleaning

☐ Take drapes down and have them dry cleaned. Movers will not take down drapes for you. Hang sheets in the windows at night.

☐ Wash the curtains.

☐ Clean any venetian blinds and light fixtures which you are not taking with you.

☐ Clean the shower curtains.

☐ Clean the kitchen appliances, stove, and utensils. Don't forget hidden traps like the crumb tray in the toaster. If you pack these dirty, they can attract bugs.

☐ Clean soap deposits on the bottom of bathroom soap dishes.

☐ Wash bedspreads and blankets.

☐ Wash potholders.

☐ If you have not already done so, clean any items which you will put in storage.

B: Household Tasks

☐ Replace any fixtures you are taking with you, such as ceiling fans, chandeliers, dimmer switches, personalized door knockers, or outdoor lighting with movement sensors.

☐ Remove the batteries from the toys and flashlights you are not using. This will prevent leaking and corrosion.

☐ Remove the kitchen towel holders, utensil holders, food racks, and other fixtures which you are taking with you.

☐ Take down pictures, mirrors, shelving, cabinets, etc. from the walls. Spackle the holes. Tape screws, bolts, and other hardware to the back of the item, or put them in a ziploc bag to go in your 'last box.'

☐ Drain the water from steam irons, humidifiers, vaporizers, water-cooled fans, and air conditioners.

☐ Place shower curtain hooks, drapery hooks, etc. together in one bag to be packed in the 'last box.'

☐ Clean the plastic silverware tray in the kitchen drawer.

☐ Put flour, sugar, and similar messy supplies in airtight plastic bags.

☐ Place rubberbands around small boxes of pins, toothpicks, hardware, index cards, etc. Secure box and basket lids.

☐ Keep on eating and drinking up! You are going to start giving food away very soon.

☐ Don't forget the hour you are giving yourself each day. It will never be more important or easier to ignore than it is now.

C: Starting To Pack

☐ Begin packing your suitcases. Appendix F offers some guidelines for what you should include.

☐ Gather up any small valuables you may have hidden or stored around the house.

☐ Collect any remaining school, medical, dental, veterinarian or other records which you will need at your destination.

☐ Empty your lockers at schools and clubs.

☐ Continue to stock up on items you will need when you get to your destination. This spares you from rushing out to buy them immediately upon your arrival (when you probably will not know the best places to shop). Pack these in a 'last box.'

☐ Set aside anything you are not packing and anything required to stay with the house. This includes warranties and manuals for installed appliances and fixtures, reset wrenches for the sink disposal, broiler pans, outdoor clothes line, paints, and similar items.

☐ If you still have items going to storage, place them all in one single area.

☐ Place grouped items in clearly separated areas. This prevents confusion later on and keeps your shipments and piles from becoming mixed up.

☐ Empty the drawers of any bureaus going into storage.

D: Children And Pets

☐ Let your children choose the activities, books, and toys they want to have with them during the move, but do limit how much they can bring. (One carry-on bag each is reasonable.)

☐ Reassure younger children that their toys and belongings will all be moved to the new house.

☐ Ask your children to help design the floor plan of their new bedroom. See Appendix A, "The Floor Plan," for more information.

☐ If you are driving, show your children a map and ask them to help plan the best route. Letting children help navigate with travel-club itineraries and maps allows them to participate in the move and helps keep them interested during the trip. (They won't ask, *How much longer?* quite so often.) Plan some road games and activities as well.

☐ Involve your children in the packing. For example, they can tape up the broken corners of their game boxes, and they can put rubberbands around each box to keep it from spilling open during the move.

☐ Have children put their shirts, coats, and dresses on hangers and button the top buttons.

☐ Make sure your kids drain the water from their squirt guns and water toys.

☐ Introduce your pet to any crate or carrier you will be using if you have not already done so. This will help your pet become accustomed to the surroundings and reduce the stress of travel.

☐ Pay attention to your pets. Animals often know that something is happening. Most animals do not like disruptions and need reassurance.

One and Two Days before You Move

A: Organizing And Packing

☐ Begin packing your car and suitcases. (See Appendix F, "Suggestions for Packing Your Car and Suitcase," for packing tips.)

☐ Check the attic and crawl spaces one more time for any items you may have stored there.

☐ If you are employing movers, clean a spare room or closet. Put everything you do not want them to pack in this area and close the door. When the movers arrive, instruct them not to pack anything in that room. Lock the room if you can. Otherwise, keep an eye on the packers to make sure they do not go into that room.

☐ Set aside any items you will need immediately upon arriving at your destination. Put them in a 'last box' or instruct the movers to do so. Appendix E is a list of recommended 'last box' items.

☐ Set the cable converter and television controller aside. The cable company will need these when it disconnects your service.

☐ Collect the cleaning supplies you will need to clean the house after the boxes and furniture have been removed. Put these where they will not get packed.

☐ Make sure each piece of luggage has an up-to-date address tag on it, working locks, extra keys, and a strap around it to prevent it from opening.

B: Appliances And Electronic Equipment

☐ Disconnect and disassemble your electronic components (stereo, turntable, amplifier, CD player, computer, printer, TV, VCR, etc). Bundle the wires and color-code them to the matching holes on the back of each unit for easier reassembly. Secure the arm of the turntable, remove the needle, and tighten the transport screws. Tighten the transport screw on your CD player, as well.

☐ Back up your computer and pack your disks or cassettes where they will not be exposed to anything magnetic. If recommended by your user's manual, park your hard drive. Put a head-protection sheet or a floppy disk in the disk drive.

☐ Use original cartons for packing your electronic equipment. If they are not available, place the items in plastic bags to keep them free from dust and dirt during packing and transportation.

☐ Allow your electronic equipment to cool down to room temperature before you move it.

☐ Remove your outdoor television antenna if you are taking it with you.

☐ Major appliances, including stoves, washers, dryers, air conditioners, refrigerators, etc., should be serviced (disconnected, emptied, and cleaned) and prepared for the move at least forty-eight hours before they are loaded on the truck.

☐ Do the laundry ahead of time. Disconnect and drain the washing machine, allowing sufficient time for it to dry. If possible, take the washer outside and tip it to drain any remaining water from the water line. Put a nylon stocking filled with a few pieces of charcoal or some baking soda inside the washer to prevent mildew. Tie the hoses and cords to the back of the machine.

☐ Clean the refrigerator. Place charcoal or baking soda inside to prevent mildew. Leave the doors open so it dries thoroughly. Empty the drainage pan under the refrigerator.

☐ If the refrigerator stays with the house, make sure the ice cube trays don't get packed.

☐ Clean the oven.

☐ Drain any water beds.

☐ Vacuum under the couch and chair cushions.

☐ Empty your vacuum cleaner, hand vacuum, and vacuum cleaner bags.

☐ Disassemble your grandfather clock, pool table, and other special pieces if you haven't already done so.

C: Yardwork And Outdoor Equipment

☐ Do the yardwork and mow the lawn for the last time. Clean your lawn mower and gardening tools.

☐ Drain the fuel and oil from your mower, edger, snowblower, string trimmer, other garden equipment, power tools, and gas cans. Disconnect any spark plugs.

☐ Hose off the outside door mats and allow both sides to dry thoroughly.

☐ Drain the water from garden hoses. When they are dry, coil the hoses and screw the ends together.

☐ Remove any hose holders, nozzles, or other items attached to the house which you are taking with you.

D: Household Tasks

☐ Take down any remaining curtains, blinds, shelves, and other removable items which are not staying behind.

☐ If you are going to take bookshelves which are anchored to the wall, pack the books and other items (or let the movers do it) *before* you remove the shelves from the wall.

☐ Inspect all rooms for utensil racks or other holders secured to walls, cabinets, or doors.

☐ Wash your sheets before you service your washer and dryer. Use a sleeping bag and air mattress, borrow a futon, or arrange to stay with friends or at a motel. If you can't make other sleeping arrangements and have already disconnected the washer and dryer, ask a neighbor to wash your sheets for you on the morning your bed gets packed.

☐ Hang clean drapes on hangers. Pack them in wardrobe cartons so they will need less attention or ironing when you unpack them.

☐ Tighten all lids, including medicines, perfumes, and bathroom items.

☐ Tape and seal jars or containers of fluids (including bathroom and cosmetic items). Place them in plastic bags in case they leak despite the tape.

☐ Also put honey, syrup, and similar leakable items in plastic bags.

☐ Tape over the openings of salt and pepper shakers, salt and baking soda boxes, and other powder containers.

☐ Discard or give away perishables and opened jars or cans of food.

☐ Empty and wash sugar bowls.

☐ Discard any containers you have used for draining fat.

☐ Close liquid soap dispensers.

☐ Scrub soap dishes and shower caddies.

☐ Empty and scrub trash cans, garbage cans, and household waste baskets. You don't want them accidentally packed with trash still in them.

☐ Set aside the toilet bowl brush. You'll appreciate it when you are doing your final cleaning. Discard the brush after using it for the last time.

☐ Give away flammables, aerosols, scrap wood, light bulbs, food and other items you don't want or can't move. Discard the rest. (Be sure to obey hazardous waste laws!)

E: Last Minute Arrangements

☐ Reconfirm your travel reservations (including kennels).

☐ Remind your babysitter of the arrangements which you made ahead of time.

☐ Make any remaining preparations for closing and transfering your bank accounts and safety deposit box. Buy travelers checks.

☐ Turn over to the next occupants any household items which they have purchased, such as carpets, drapes, and blinds. If you leave them in the house, make sure they don't get packed.

☐ Arrange to borrow a vacuum or broom from one of your neighbors for last minute cleaning.

☐ If you will need a ride to the airport, make arrangements with a friend, a neighbor, or a taxi company.

☐ Plan healthy snacks for your family and yourself on moving day. If you will be eating lunch at home, use disposable plates and cups.

☐ Get some styrofoam cups, sugar, milk, and coffee for friends and/or movers on moving day.

☐ Give a relative and a neighbor your itinerary and phone numbers to contact you during your trip in case of an emergency.

☐ If your home will be vacant after you leave, let the police and your neighbors know.

Professional Packing And Moving

A: Preparations

☐ Get up early on the day the packers will arrive. You'll appreciate the extra couple of hours you have allowed yourself to get organized.

☐ Plan to be up late on both packing and loading days.

☐ If your other shipments have not already been picked up or taken to storage, group them in separate areas.

☐ Make sure that all items have been removed from the attic and crawl spaces. Movers are not required to enter areas which do not have permanent stairs, have unfinished floors, are not adequately lighted, or lack the necessary headroom for standing up.

☐ Collect everything that the packers should not touch and put it all in a shut-off area, such as a sealed-off closet or bathroom. You will be telling the packers not to enter the area. Among these isolated items are:

  • Whatever you will be carrying with you.
  • Items which will stay with the house.
  • Items which will be stored, if they have not yet been picked up or delivered.
  • Any remaining flammables, aerosols, or other items you will be giving away.
  • Items for express shipment overseas if they have not yet been picked up.

- ☐ Put professional items together in a separate area.
- ☐ Make another separate pile of 'last box' items.
- ☐ Complete Your Declared Valuation Statement before packing and loading begins.
- ☐ Don't leave jewelry, cash, or other valuables unguarded. Lock them in your car or leave them at a neighbor's house.
- ☐ Don't make any appointments outside the house or run any errands while the packers or movers are working unless there is a responsible adult at your house to supervise them.
- ☐ Make sure the dishes are washed, dried, and put away in the cabinets.
- ☐ Remove light bulbs from lamps and the batteries from flashlights so they won't break, corrode, or leak.
- ☐ Empty the trash before packers arrive. Otherwise, they might accidentally pack it.
- ☐ Put a first aid kit in your sealed-off room where it will not get packed.
- ☐ If your refrigerator has been cleaned and disconnected, use a cooler (your neighbor's, if possible) to hold your food and beverages for the next day or so.
- ☐ Make sure you have removed all the dishes from your dishwasher.
- ☐ Keep children and pets out of the way when packers and movers are working.
- ☐ Reassure younger children. It can be very confusing to watch all of your worldly goods being packed into boxes by strangers.
- ☐ Keep all stairways clear.
- ☐ Set aside some large trash bags for clean up.
- ☐ Have coffee and doughnuts available for the packers. Offer soft drinks in the afternoon.
- ☐ Your most important task will be to supervise the packing and loading of your goods. So be prepared.

B: Instructions for Packers and Movers

☐ If the packers or movers haven't arrived by 9:00 AM, call their office.

☐ As soon as packers arrive, walk them through your house. Show them the room or rooms you have sealed off. Explain that there is nothing in the room for them to pack and ask them not to enter.

☐ Make formal requests to the packers through their foreman or whoever is in charge of the crew. You may not need to practice this formality, but until you learn otherwise, assume that there are rules which you should respect.

☐ Request that the packers label all of the boxes of professional items which you have set aside as *Pro Items*. Ask that they make the same notation on the inventory sheets.

☐ Request packers to label boxes accurately. Ask them to specify on the box and inventory sheet any important item they may have packed in it. This will make the retrieval of microwaves, clock radios, and other useful items easier at your destination.

☐ If you have not set them aside in separate areas, point out the items which you have designated for storage shipments, express shipments, and other special treatment. Emphasize that these should not be packed.

☐ Show the packers items which should be packed in the 'last box.'

☐ If more than one day is required for packing, ask the packers not to dismantle the beds until the actual moving day. Likewise, request that bedroom lights and sleeping bags be packed on the last day.

☐ Verify that the packers will *roll* all your rugs. (Folding rugs can do a lot of damage.)

☐ Request mirror cartons for your pictures and mirrors.

☐ Request a styrofoam washer block to secure the agitator in your washing machine.

☐ Tell the packers to ask you if they are unsure about something. Be very explicit so that nothing is packed erroneously.

☐ Packers are required to use new packing materials and arrive with a swept out van.

☐ If you are not satisfied with any aspect of the packing, call your moving representative.

☐ Only you can supervise the packers and movers to ensure that they are doing a good job. If you see something you don't like, speak up politely. You are paying the company a lot of money and you have the right to insist that its employees pack and load your household goods properly.

C: Inventory Sheets

☐ Instruct the packers to describe silver, expensive antiques, and other items of high value separately on inventory sheets. Be able to declare a value for each item. Have the value recorded on the inventory sheets. (You should already have taken photos and had appraisals done).

☐ Make sure that any damage notations on inventory sheets are accurate and precise. (For example, damage descriptions should note *exactly* where an item is nicked or scratched.) Inventory sheets should also indicate when an item is new or in extremely good condition.

☐ If you disagree with a damage description, note your disagreement on the inventory sheet.

☐ Accompany the movers during inventory. Check their notations and make your own if necessary. Verify that everything has an inventory number.

☐ Make sure professional items are listed as *Pro Items* on the inventory sheet and the boxes. The military and some businesses consider professional items to be separate from your household shipment and do not include the weight of these items in the weight of your total shipment. This exclusion is particularly helpful if your household shipment has a weight limit. Also, any item marked *Pro Item* can be taken directly to your study, home office, or any other room you have designated in your new home.

D: Loading

☐ Get up early to allow yourself time before the movers arrive.

☐ Inspect the van and crates for cleanliness.

☐ If the weather is bad, movers are required to cover your belongings while they carry them between your home and the moving van.

☐ Verify that the van has been weighed with *full* fuel tanks before your goods are loaded. If the truck is tanked and weighed after loading is done, the weight of the fuel—approximately 200 gallons at 7 or so pounds per gallon—will be added to the total weight of your shipment.

☐ Movers will dismantle the beds, two-piece bureaus, kitchen and dining room tables, pianos, and other large items. Ask them to attach screws, castors, and other hardware to the proper piece of furniture or else to give them to you for proper labeling and bagging.

☐ Mattresses and box springs must be put in mattress cartons.

☐ If your bureaus are not too full, they will be loaded with the contents intact. (It certainly is convenient to find your clothes in their usual spot when your household goods are delivered!)

☐ If possible during loading, one person should supervise from the door to insure that each item has an inventory number on it and that everything is loaded satisfactorily.

☐ Make sure your furniture is properly wrapped before loading and padded well in the van to prevent rubbing.

☐ Instruct movers to load rugs, rug pads, the vacuum, and the items designated as 'last box' after everything else has been loaded. Rugs and pads go last so they can be unloaded and rolled out in their designated rooms before the rest of your household goods are unloaded.

☐ Load the vacuum cleaner last so you can sweep and vacuum out each room as it is emptied.

☐ Take care of any loose ends by phone before your telephone service is disconnected.

☐ Pack your own car (see Appendix F).

☐ Give away left over food and refrigerated items.

☐ Have coffee available for the movers. It is a nice gesture. Movers appreciate it, and it does create a better atmosphere and working relationship. You can also offer to buy them lunch. It's a long, trying day, and it helps keep the movers happy. (This can pay off, too, when you suddenly discover that you need to ask the movers to help you do something you should have done earlier.) Budget for this—it's well worth the expense.

E: Before The Movers Leave

- ☐ Take one last look through the house, checking closets, shelves, medicine cabinets, drawers, attics, crawl spaces, backs of doors, shed walls, etc. for anything the movers have overlooked.

- ☐ If you need some extra boxes to pack your personal items, ask the movers to leave some with you. Otherwise, the movers are required to remove all of their packing materials and debris before leaving.

- ☐ Note any damage caused by the movers on your inventory sheets and those of the driver. When you sign each inventory sheet and the Bill of Lading, add a statement such as: "Subject to final inspection of all items for damage or loss."

- ☐ Look over the Bill of Lading carefully. This is a form stating the terms and conditions under which your goods will be moved. It serves as your receipt for the shipment. Make sure it is accurate. Review all details listed on the Bill of Lading. Don't sign it unless everything is correct, including the valuation coverage. Review all delivery details (address, telephone numbers, schedule, etc.) for accuracy.

- ☐ Make sure your Declared Valuation Statement is in order. This should have been completed before packing and loading began.

- ☐ Inventory sheets list everything you are shipping. These are extremely important documents, and they should be safeguarded. Make sure you have been given a signed copy of each inventory page. Both you and the driver are required to sign each inventory sheet.

☐ Before the carrier leaves with your household goods, make sure that you have the following information:

- The bill-of-lading number, which is printed on the Bill of Lading. This is the reference number for your shipment. You will need to refer to it any time you call the carrier.
- The name of the origin agent (moving company) along with the telephone number and name of a contact person in the organization.
- The driver's name and the vehicle unit number.
- The name of the destination agent, as well as its telephone number and a contact person.

☐ Make sure that the carrier has your correct destination address, a contact telephone number, and an alternate telephone number. If the mover cannot contact you within so many hours of the arrival of your shipment, your household goods will be put into storage at your expense.

☐ Give the driver a local map of your destination if the delivery location is not clearly visible on a regular city map.

☐ After it departs, the truck will stop at a weighing station. You have the right to accompany the truck to verify the official weight of your shipment.

☐ Request that a representative of the moving company notify you as soon as the exact cost of the move is known. Make sure the company has telephone numbers where you can be contacted.

☐ If you need to communicate with the moving company at any time, refer to the bill-of-lading number which you will find on your copy of the bill of lading.

☐ If you are pleased with the work the driver has done, you can send his company a letter of recommendation and you can request him for your next move.

F: After The Movers Leave

☐ Finish cleaning up.

☐ Place trash bags at the curb or ask a neighbor to set them out on trash day.

☐ Record the gas, electric, and water meter readings and keep a copy. Notify the appropriate utilities.

☐ Make sure that all the doors and windows are locked.

☐ Leave your forwarding address so new residents can forward your mail, if necessary.

☐ Return keys to the landlord, apartment manager, or realtor.

☐ Spend an hour on yourself.

Arriving At Your Destination

A: First Things

☐ Contact your realtor, landlord, or housing office.

☐ If you arrive before your household goods, check in at a previously reserved hotel or motel.

☐ If you are being moved, notify the destination agent listed on the Bill of Lading as soon as you arrive. Give the company a telephone number where you can be reached for notification of delivery. This is important. If the destination agent is unable to contact you within a set number of hours after your shipment arrives, your goods will be unloaded and placed in storage at your expense.

☐ If you have young children, make child-care arrangements for move-in day.

☐ Plan fire-evacuation routes for your new home and practice them with your family as soon as you can get in.

☐ Finalize the floor plans you made after your househunting trip (see Part 1C and Appendix A). Now that you are actually in the house, you can see the rooms and make any changes you want to your plans before the furniture comes in. Don't wait until after your things are in the house.

☐ If your household goods are being moved professionally, consult your floor plans and make pencil notes on your inventory sheets about the rooms in which boxes and items of furniture should be placed. This will make unloading faster and less confusing.

B: Household Tasks

☐ Change the door locks and make duplicate keys.

☐ Check the plumbing and heating, the electrical outlets, appliances, smoke detectors, etc. to make sure they are all in good working order.

☐ Shop for cleaning supplies, replacement parts, washer and dryer hoses, dryer vents, lightbulbs, and other items that you may need—refer to the list you made as you were preparing for your move.

☐ Purchase a few groceries—bread, peanut butter, jelly, drinks, cereal, milk, etc.—for move-in day.

☐ If your home needs cleaning, do it before your household goods are unloaded.

☐ Do any needed minor work, especially if your shipment hasn't arrived yet. Chores like painting, for example, are much easier to do without furniture in house.

☐ Arrange for major appliances to be connected if you are unsure of the proper procedures.

☐ If you want to line your kitchen cabinets and drawers with contact paper, do it before your kitchen items are unpacked.

C: Business, Finance, And Attractions

☐ Inform the local post office about the day you want mail delivery to start. Ask if any mail is already being held for you.

☐ Visit your bank and open your accounts if you didn't open them ahead of time.

☐ Contact your insurance company, if necessary.

☐ Confirm the gas, electric, and water turn-on dates with the utility company.

☐ Before confirming your telephone installation, check to see that the phone outlets are placed correctly in your home. (A floor outlet where you want a wall phone won't do you much good). Arranging for changes to be made at the time of installation will save you extra charges later.

☐ Write local emergency numbers on the telephones.

☐ Arrange for fuel delivery, trash pick up, newspaper delivery, diaper delivery, etc.

☐ Locate the nearest hospitals to your new home and identify the best routes to them on your map.

D: Children And Pets

☐ Have your children memorize their new address and telephone number as soon as you arrive, if not earlier. Consider giving younger children identification cards or bracelets to carry.

☐ Find reliable baby sitters by talking to neighbors or contacting local colleges and high schools. Local community associations or church groups may also maintain lists of babysitters.

☐ Enroll your children in school. Show your kids their new school and arrange for them to have a tour before they start classes.

☐ If school is in session, have your children start attending right away. Introduce them to their new teachers and assure them that the teachers will help them if they need anything. Ask the teachers to assign them a 'buddy' from the class to walk them through their first day of school.

☐ The first day at a new school can be very worrysome and full of stress. Talk to your children about the new routine. Reassure them that you will be waiting for them after school.

☐ Get licenses for your pets and make sure they have address and identification tags on their collars.

Moving In

9

A: Preparations

☐ Plan on a late day!

☐ Tape your floor plans for each room on their respective doors.

☐ If movers will be unloading your goods, the notes on your inventory sheets should indicate the rooms where each item should go. Mark the items and the cartons you want to open first, including the 'last carton.' Indicate on your inventory sheets that these these items should be placed in a separate area.

☐ Plug in your telephone (it should be in your 'last box' or in your car) and write your new phone number on it. Also tape a list of emergency numbers to your phone.

☐ Make the beds and plug in some lights in the bedrooms as soon as you can. When you are exhausted and ready for bed, you'll be glad you have already done this.

☐ Put sheets over the windows temporarily if there are no drapes or window shades.

☐ Remember to let the television and other electrical items warm up or cool down to room temperature before you turn them on.

B: If The Movers Unload

☐ If you are paying movers yourself, you will have to pay the driver in full before the movers will start to unload your goods. Moving companies accept travelers checks, money orders, and cashier's checks. Some may also accept credit cards, but you will need to verify this in advance.

☐ Movers will usually try to unload everything from their van in one day. If you have a large shipment, request extra movers to help with the unloading in order to avoid an extra-long day. Remember that the movers will also need time to unpack if your binding estimate includes unpacking your household goods. They may have to come back the next day to finish the job if it is too late once the van is unloaded.

☐ Walk the movers through the house or apartment. Point out the floor plans which you have taped to the door of each room. Explain that it is important for these plans to be followed. Take as much time as you need to explain your floor plans in detail. Ask the movers to refer to the floor plan when they place items in the room and to check with you if they don't understand something.

☐ Movers should unload rugs and pads first and place them in their proper locations before they bring in any furniture or boxes.

☐ As soon as your rugs and pads are down, line the entryway and high-traffic areas with paper or plastic runners.

☐ Next, movers should bring in your 'last boxes.' Find a secure place where these can be placed and unpacked.

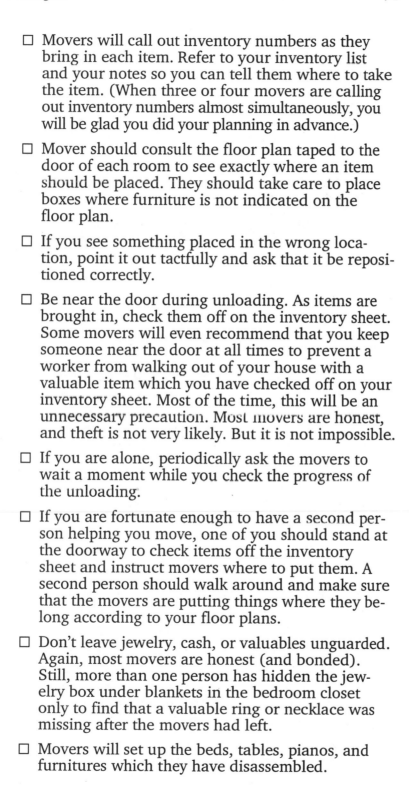

☐ Movers will call out inventory numbers as they bring in each item. Refer to your inventory list and your notes so you can tell them where to take the item. (When three or four movers are calling out inventory numbers almost simultaneously, you will be glad you did your planning in advance.)

☐ Mover should consult the floor plan taped to the door of each room to see exactly where an item should be placed. They should take care to place boxes where furniture is not indicated on the floor plan.

☐ If you see something placed in the wrong location, point it out tactfully and ask that it be repositioned correctly.

☐ Be near the door during unloading. As items are brought in, check them off on the inventory sheet. Some movers will even recommend that you keep someone near the door at all times to prevent a worker from walking out of your house with a valuable item which you have checked off on your inventory sheet. Most of the time, this will be an unnecessary precaution. Most movers are honest, and theft is not very likely. But it is not impossible.

☐ If you are alone, periodically ask the movers to wait a moment while you check the progress of the unloading.

☐ If you are fortunate enough to have a second person helping you move, one of you should stand at the doorway to check items off the inventory sheet and instruct movers where to put them. A second person should walk around and make sure that the movers are putting things where they belong according to your floor plans.

☐ Don't leave jewelry, cash, or valuables unguarded. Again, most movers are honest (and bonded). Still, more than one person has hidden the jewelry box under blankets in the bedroom closet only to find that a valuable ring or necklace was missing after the movers had left.

☐ Movers will set up the beds, tables, pianos, and furnitures which they have disassembled.

☐ Inspect your furniture and boxes for visible damage as they are brought in. Make notes of any damage on your inventory sheet and on the driver's copy. Ask the movers to open boxes that appear damaged. Make notations of any damage before the movers leave.

☐ Report any damage to the destination agent immediately. Put any damaged items in one area and prepare to file a claim. Obtain claim forms from your moving representative.

☐ Don't repair anything yet or throw anything out until a the claim has been filed and inspections completed. See Appendix D for guidelines on filing an insurance claim.

☐ You may be able to have repairs made to necessary items before your claims are fully processed if the insurance company approves. See Appendix D for further information.

☐ If your company is paying for the move, it should have a representative assigned to handle damage claims. If you are paying for the move, contact your insurance company and have its representative look at the damage. Consult with your insurance company about the proper procedure for filing a claim.

☐ Don't sign the driver's copy of the inventory sheet unless all of your boxes and items are accounted for. If something is missing, note it on both the driver's copy and your copy of the inventory before you sign the inventory sheets.

☐ Don't sign the Bill of Lading until missing and visibly damaged items are noted on the form. You cannot refuse to sign the Bill of Lading, but you will find it more difficult to prove a claim later if you do not make note of damages now.

☐ Make sure the carrier's agent (usually the foreman or driver) signs and dates all copies legibly and leaves you a copy of all paperwork.

☐ If the delivery of your household goods was beyond the quoted time frame, ask the movers, your company, or whoever is responsible for the delay about being reimbursed for your reasonable out-of-pocket expenses. Ask the moving company to send you the necessary forms and instructions for submitting your claim.

☐ Have styrofoam cups and coffee available for you and the movers.

☐ Write a letter of appreciation to the moving company if you were pleased with its service.

C: If The Movers Unpack

☐ Always have movers unpack for you if it is in your contract. At the very least, have them unpack your kitchen and dining room. These rooms may be more cluttered initially, but having them unpacked is a good idea because:

- It will save you a lot of time, especially with the dishes and glassware, each of which has been wrapped individually.
- Kitchenware can be fragile. If it is unpacked, more of the damage becomes evident and can be noted before movers leave.
- It is much easier to put everything away if it has been unwrapped for you.
- The movers will remove empty boxes and paper. Flattening boxes and disposing of them yourself can be time-consuming.

☐ Note any damage for your insurance claim.

☐ If you are unpacking the shipment yourself, ask the destination agent to come back and remove the boxes and paper for you. There might be an extra charge for this service.

☐ See the next section for tips if you will be unpacking yourself.

D: If You Unload
And Unpack

☐ Before you begin to unload, go over the floor plans for each room. Make sure that you place boxes and furniture with the floor plans in mind. After all, if you stack book boxes or wardrobe cartons where the bed is supposed to go, you will frustrate one major purpose of your floor plan.

☐ Unload rugs and pads and place them in their proper places before any furniture is brought into the house.

☐ After the rugs are down, lay paper in the entryway so your rugs and floors won't get too dirty.

☐ Unpack and set up children's rooms early. This will help them feel settled and comfortable in their new surroundings.

☐ Assign your children small jobs that are appropriate for their age level (unpacking toys, throwing out wrapping papers, etc.).

☐ Unpack your breakables over a box. You'll be less likely to break something if you should drop it.

☐ Save a few boxes (book boxes for storing books and wardrobe cartons for winter coats, blankets, and similar items). Put some mothballs in those boxes in which you are storing clothes. Place all boxes off the basement or garage floors to avoid moisture damage.

E: After You've Moved In

- ☐ Take a deep breath and relax! (For a minute anyway!)

- ☐ Make a quick trip to the store for any items you may need.

- ☐ If you decide to go out to eat, leave a light and a radio on and lock up to prevent theft.

- ☐ Remove any movers' inventory stickers unless you are willing to see stickers on your furniture for years to come. (This is a particularly good job for children. I pay my children a token amount for each sticker they remove. Not only do my children actively hunt for them, but they also stay busy while we unpack.)

- ☐ Keep on taking time for yourself.

International Moves

A: Preparations

☐ Apply for passports through the post office or, in some areas, your local court house. The entire process can take up to three months, so begin as soon as possible. Call for prices and budget for this—it can be quite expensive.

☐ When you apply for a new passport, you will need a certified copy of your birth certificate and two passport photos.

☐ If you have had a passport issued to you in the past, you will need your old passport itself or a copy of it with the passport number.

☐ Keep a copy of your passport application until your passport is issued to you.

☐ Make a photocopy of your passport and put it in a safe place, apart from your original. This will facilitate the replacement of a lost or stolen passport.

☐ Military and state department personnel along with their dependents may be issued a no-fee or diplomatic passport. If you also want a tourist passport for travelling to other countries, you must obtain it separately.

☐ Find out from the office where you applied for your passport if a visa will also be required by your country of destination. If so, you will need to keep your visa with your passport when you enter the country.

☐ Request information about your destination from the country's embassy or consulate in Washington D.C. Also write to the American Embassy in the foreign country and ask for any information it can provide.

☐ The U.S. Department of State issues periodic advisories about the nations of the world. The most recent copies of these advisories are available in libraries, travel agencies, travel health clinics, and directly from the State Department. They can also be viewed on computerized databases, such as CompuServe.

☐ For more information (for both civilians and military personnel), call **OTIS** (Overseas Transfer Information Service), Bureau of Naval Personnel, Washington, D.C. 20370. Call toll free at 800-327-8197 or call collect at 703-697-6621 or 6634 (**OTIS** will accept the charges). **OTIS** offers information on auto shipments, pets, government and civilian housing, schools, spouse employment and job opportunities, medical and dental facilities, and other matters of concern.

☐ Visit your local library for books and video tapes available. Read up on the country's protocol, customs, manners and beliefs.

☐ Contact residents of the country who may be living in your area. Ask them about their country and get as many tips as they are willing to share. Doing a little research can help you prepare for some of the little shocks. You won't be quite as surprised when you move to Japan, for example, if you know before you arrive that you may be required by law to pay one year of apartment rent in advance.

☐ Ask that a local newspaper from your destination country be sent to you.

☐ Brush up on current events and national affairs in your new country. Obtain a working knowledge of the new political system.

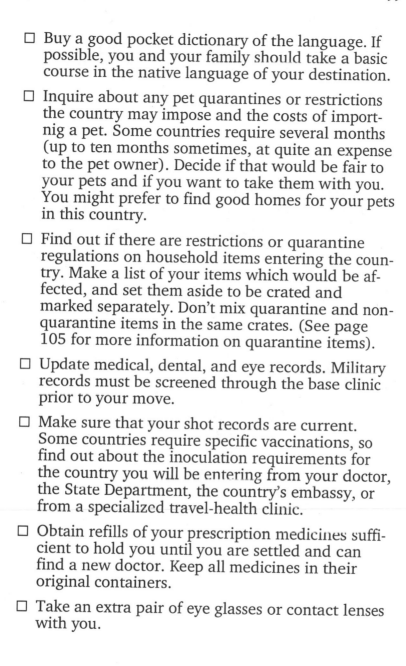

☐ Buy a good pocket dictionary of the language. If possible, you and your family should take a basic course in the native language of your destination.

☐ Inquire about any pet quarantines or restrictions the country may impose and the costs of importnig a pet. Some countries require several months (up to ten months sometimes, at quite an expense to the pet owner). Decide if that would be fair to your pets and if you want to take them with you. You might prefer to find good homes for your pets in this country.

☐ Find out if there are restrictions or quarantine regulations on household items entering the country. Make a list of your items which would be affected, and set them aside to be crated and marked separately. Don't mix quarantine and non-quarantine items in the same crates. (See page 105 for more information on quarantine items).

☐ Update medical, dental, and eye records. Military records must be screened through the base clinic prior to your move.

☐ Make sure that your shot records are current. Some countries require specific vaccinations, so find out about the inoculation requirements for the country you will be entering from your doctor, the State Department, the country's embassy, or from a specialized travel-health clinic.

☐ Obtain refills of your prescription medicines sufficient to hold you until you are settled and can find a new doctor. Keep all medicines in their original containers.

☐ Take an extra pair of eye glasses or contact lenses with you.

B: Documentation

☐ Find out when your current driver's license and vehicle registration expire. Take renewal applications with you, if necessary.

☐ Apply for an international drivers license if you will need one.

☐ Obtain a driver's manual from the country you will be entering. Request one from the country's embassy or from an overseas sponsor. Study it along with local road maps while you are en route.

☐ Contact your insurance companies and find out how to maintain coverage while you are overseas. Some insurance companies do not offer auto insurance coverage overseas. However, most will still cover your household goods and personal property.

☐ Medical and dental insurance may also be affected by your move. Find out how your claims will be handled. Don't be surprised if you have to pay bills up front and submit claims for reimbursement. Budget for monthly medical expenses if you will be required to pay fees up front.

☐ Get a large supply of your medical and dental claim forms to take with you. Also find out the proper address for submitting claims while you are overseas.

☐ If you are in the military, make sure that your military and dependent I.D.s will not expire before you return to this country.

☐ Keep in your possession or in a safe deposit box official copies of your marriage license, birth certificates, divorce papers, adoption papers, insurance policies, appraisals of valuables, social security cards, stocks and bonds, coins and stamps, and any other personal documents which can't be replaced.

☐ Leave a Power-of-Attorney and a current will with a relative, a responsible friend, or a lawyer. Appoint that person to act legally on your behalf while you are overseas in the event of an emergency. Keep copies of these documents with you.

☐ If you want another person—even your spouse—to have access to information about your life insurance policy, you will need to authorize it in writing to the insurance company.

☐ Keep at least one checking account in the United States. You will need a domestic account to pay bills, order items, renew subscriptions, and transact certain other types of business.

☐ Apply for an absentee ballot through your current voter registration office.

C: Vehicles

☐ Get information on importing and exporting vehicles into your new country. Contact a sponsor, the company which is relocating you, or the State Department.

☐ OTIS (see page 98, above) is the best source of information if you are planning to ship your vehicles. **OTIS** can provide current information on regulations, pollution control devices, vehicle shipment arrangements, required documentation, etc. **OTIS** will be able to advise you if you will be required to remove your catalytic converter; if your country doesn't sell unleaded gas; if there are age limits for importing vehicles; and if your country has special restrictions which might affect you. (Some countries, for example, prohibit individuals from importing black cars, which are reserved for officials.)

☐ Some countries may not allow you to bring your own car. Before you leave for such a nation, apply for a pre-approved loan from your bank or credit union for a car purchase overseas. Get the institution's telefax number to facilitate the actual purchase while overseas.

☐ You may only be allowed to ship one car. Decide if you want to purchase a second car after you arrive. Budget for this, including registration and insurance. You can also arrange for a pre-approved loan if you plan to buy a second car overseas.

☐ Keep your car ownership and registration papers with you during the move.

☐ Ask your insurance company if it recommends extra coverage while shipping an automobile.

☐ You may not ship a vehicle if it has a lien against it or if it is leased.

☐ When you begin shipping your car, arrive at the dock with a minimal amount of fuel in your gas tank. Most of the fuel will be drained before your car is loaded.

☐ Remove CB radios and tape decks before shipping. Leave the luggage rack in the trunk—you will need it when you arrive.

☐ Find out about car insurance requirements in your new country and how to obtain coverage.

☐ Even if your present auto insurance policy will not cover you overseas, ask your auto insurance company to issue you a 'good driver certificate' if you have had a good driving record over the last several years. This may qualify you for a discount on your insurance in some countries.

☐ If you have an auto club membership card, bring it with you. You may qualify for an additional discount when applying for membership in a reciprocal automobile association.

☐ If you are selling your car or cars, cancel your auto insurance as soon as your vehicles are sold.

☐ If your car cannot be serviced at your destination and you do not want to sell it, stock up on tires, wipers, hoses, and other necessary parts. Budget for this. Find a reliable parts supplier in this country who will ship you any parts you need.

D: Organization

☐ Go through your household goods. Sort them according to shipment type:

- Storage shipment.
- Express shipment (see section F, below).
- Household goods shipment.
- Professional items.
- 'Last box' items (see Appendix E).
- Quarantine items (see below).
- Suitcases.

☐ If you are being relocated overseas, find out if your employer has a weight allowance for your household goods.

☐ If your shipment will be crated, inspect the crates carefully as soon as you obtain them. If they are not sturdy, if they have knotholes missing, if they are warped, or if they don't seal properly, the crates will not be accepted by customs. Your household goods may then have to be re-crated before being shipped by air or by sea. Call your moving representative and refuse any crates which are not in acceptable condition.

☐ If something in your household goods shipment is too large to fit into a standard crate, you or your movers can custom-build a crate for it. Call it to their attention during your pre-inspection.

☐ If you have a contact overseas, find out if you will be able to buy used converters, transformers, appliances, and other necessities. Ask for a list of things you will and will not need to bring with you.

☐ Don't buy any electrical appliances until you find out about the voltage differences between here and there.

☐ The more information you gather, the easier it will be to decide what is appropriate to ship with your household goods and what should be put into storage. (As a personal example, before we moved to Australia, we discovered that most homes had wall-to-wall carpeting. We were able to put all of our rugs in storage. Had we not learned this ahead of time, we would have been hard-pressed to store these rugs in our home.)

☐ Know the customs regulations for the country you will be entering. Some items, including certain types of foods, may not be allowed to enter the country. Customs will confiscate them and you will not be reimbursed.

☐ Find out if any items will require inspection or heat or disinfectant treatment and if any other items will be quarantined upon entry. Separate these items from your household goods. See that they are packed in a separate crate marked *Quarantine* on the outside. Customs will inspect these upon their arrival in country.

The requirements of each country are different. Nevertheless, some of the items which might have to be inspected include:

- Food items.
- Baskets.
- Antique furniture.
- Bamboo and cane items.
- Goods made wholly or partly of wood from Asia or Southeast Asia.
- Straw articles.
- Dried flowers.
- Sphagnum moss.
- Christmas decorations (such as pine cones).
- Shells.
- Native artifacts.
- Bikes.
- Garden tools.
- Plant pots.
- Outdoor furniture and equipment.

☐ Make a list of items to stock up on—those which are either not available or are very expensive overseas. Start purchasing a few items each month to ship with your household goods. Give a list of these items to your relatives and friends for "care-package" ideas.

☐ Look over your luggage and determine if you need to acquire additional pieces for your trip. Budget for this.

☐ Ask your overseas sponsor, if you have one, or some other contact to make hotel reservations for your arrival.

E: Details, Details, Details

☐ Budget for different wardrobe needs, if necessary.

☐ Apply for an international telephone calling card. If you can't get one which is honored world-wide, make sure you get one which is accepted in your destination country. Contact your local telephone company for information.

☐ Apply for an internationally accepted credit card for overseas purchases.

☐ Make sure you have the owner's manuals and warranties for any appliances, equipment, or machinery you are taking with you, along with with addresses for obtaining replacement parts.

☐ You will need to obtain transformers, converters, and TV and electrical items because of differences in voltage and broadcast formats. These can be quite expensive. Unless your electric clocks, turntables, Christmas tree lights, etc. are dual voltage, however, they will not work. Your computer will need a transformer. Refrigerators, washing machines, dryers, and items with motors should be put into storage or sold.

☐ You may be able to run sixty-Hertz motors, timers, and other electrical items on fifty Hertz of power. However, they will run slower and hotter, which may reduce their life expectancy.

☐ When you return home, your household goods will need to clear customs. Before you make any large purchases overseas, find out which items are restricted and which you will have to pay duty on.

☐ Keep a list of those purchases you make abroad (such as electrical items) which you plan to sell before you return home. Keep a record of purchase prices, as well.

☐ Baggage on overseas flights is limited. Mail a package to yourself at your overseas address (or to a contact's address) with clothes and other items you will need upon arrival but not en route. This is especially appropriate if you are moving into a different season. Keep your postage receipt. This is a moving expense which you can report to your employer or use as a deduction on your income tax return.

☐ Carry at least one voltage converter with you so you can use your hair dryer, electric razor, or other electrical item in your hotel or temporary lodging.

☐ Subscribe to the Sunday newspaper of your choice from back home and have it mailed to you overseas. News coverage abroad can be very inadequate.

☐ If you belong to a country club, bring your membership card. Some clubs have reciprocity.

☐ If you will have an APO or FPO address overseas, subscribe to mail-order catalogs of companies which will mail to an APO or FPO address. Get extra order forms and bring their credit cards with you.

☐ Bring camera-film mailers with you if you have APO or FPO access. In most countries it is very expensive to have film developed.

☐ Get a metric conversion card to carry with you if you are uncomfortable with the metric system.

☐ Start purchasing small gifts which you can use to thank your sponsor or anyone else who shows you hospitality.

☐ Rent a safety deposit box for any important papers you decide not to take with you. Authorize someone responsible to have access if the need arises.

☐ If your household goods are going overseas by ship, carry with you the name of the ship, the port of departure and arrival, and the approximate arrival date. This will facilitate any inquiries.

F: Express Shipments

(An express shipment should contain items you will need immediately upon arrival before your household goods arrive. It is usually packed prior to your regular household goods and shipped to arrive at your destination at the same time as you arrive.)

☐ If your household goods will be shipped by air express rather than by sea or ground, you probably will not need an express shipment.

☐ An express shipment is a separate shipment. However, the weight of the express shipment is considered part of your total household goods shipment.

☐ Among the contents of your express shipment you might include:

- Selected professional books, professional items, and clothes which you will need immediately.
- Pots, pans, dishes, and silverware.
- Kitchen utensils (manual can opener, knives, spatula, large spoons, measuring cups and spoons).
- A microwave (which will work with a transformer).
- A coffee pot or teapot for boiling water.
- Coffee, creamer, sugar, tea, salt & pepper and spices.
- Paper plates, silverware, cups.
- Paper towels, toilet paper, tissues.
- Soap, soap dishes, dish soap, laundry detergent.
- Dish towels.
- Trash bags, kitchen bags, freezer bags, and baggies.
- A shower curtain and a bath mat.
- Shampoo and toilet articles.

- Wash cloths, towels, sheets, pillowcases, pillows, and blankets.
- Infant care items.
- An iron and an ironing board.
- A television set.
- A portable radio.
- A flashlight.
- A small tool kit (metric and standard).
- A tape measure.
- Your phone book.
- Gifts, wrapping paper, ribbon, bows, tape, and scissors.
- Paper, pens, stationery, and envelopes.
- A small sewing kit.
- Batteries.
- Toys for children.
- A small table lamp.
- Résumés.

☐ If you need to use some of the above items right up until moving day, you will not be able to include them in your express shipment. Put them in a box and mail them to yourself at your overseas address (or that of a contact person). They should be waiting for you when you arrive in the new country.

☐ Keep your postage receipts. These are moving expenses for which you may be reimbursed by your company. If not, they are still tax-deductible expenses.

G: Arriving

☐ Arrive with an open mind! You're not in Kansas anymore.

☐ Exchange only as much money as you need to at the airport, where the exchange rate is not very favorable. Exchange more at a bank. You can also order foreign currency from your local bank about two weeks before you leave. Check the exchange rate—it may vary.

☐ As soon as you arrive, register with the U.S. Consulate or Embassy nearest you. It can help you with problems or questions you may have. In an emergency, your relatives can get a message to you by way of the consulate or embassy.

☐ If you are not near a foreign service outpost, make sure your relatives know how to contact you through the Red Cross in an emergency. The Red Cross will need your full name, Social Security number, and the complete name and address of your home or business.

☐ If you lose your passport, report the loss both to the nearest U.S. passport office or the nearest U.S. Embassy or Consulate and to the local police. You will need a copy of the police report when you apply for a duplicate passport.

☐ Be careful before you sign a house rental or lease agreement. If possible, have a legal officer in the area consulate review it for you.

☐ Immediately begin taking advantage of your chance to live and learn in a foreign country. Find out what the country has to offer. Plan to see as much of the country as you can during your stay. You may not get an opportunity like this again.

□

After You Have Settled In

A: Taking Care Of Business

☐ Save all of your move-related receipts, and keep careful records of your expenditures and gas mileage. Your tax advisor or accountant can advise you as to which of these expenses can be deducted on your tax returns. (Include receipts for your househunting trip, any temporary living expenses, the costs associated with buying and selling homes, and any other expense which you would not have incurred had you not moved).

☐ Contact the local motor vehicle department for regulations on car registration and driver licensing.

☐ Call City Hall for voter registration information.

☐ Property and estate laws may be different in your new location. Meet with a local lawyer or accountant if you have any questions about property ownership and transfer, inheritances, trusts, wills, estates, or taxes.

☐ Introduce yourself to your neighbors. Break the ice by asking them about the trash collection schedule. You can also ask them to refer you to doctors, dentists, childcare providers, hairdressers, stores, and other services.

☐ Contact the Welcome Wagon, Newcomers Club, the YMCA or YWCA, and other community and church groups in your area.

☐ Get out and enjoy your new home town. Explore...Get involved...Make the most of it! Start right away.

B: Children And Pets

☐ Watch your children and pets closely until they are familiar with the neighborhood.

☐ Make sure your children have memorized their new address and phone number. Younger children can carry identification cards or wear identification bracelets until they no longer need them.

☐ Be sensitive to any difficulties your children may be having at school and elsewhere. Adjustments and changes can be frustrating. Contact their teachers if you have any concerns.

☐ Encourage your children to participate in sports and extra-curricular activities. This is an excellent way for them to meet friends with similar interests.

APPENDIX A

The Floor Plan

Perhaps the greatest time and labor saving device for anyone moving to a new home is the floor plan. This is so easy to make and so useful to have that I strongly recommend one to everyone who is moving.

Have you ever found that a room was much smaller than you thought it would be once you started putting your furniture in it? This is the worst time to discover that you have overestimated the space available to you.

This unwelcome surprise is totally unnecessary. All you need to prevent it is a home-furniture-and-appliance template (available in most stationary and department stores), a tape measure, some graph paper, and a little time.

As soon as you know you will be moving, go through each room in your home and measure the exact dimensions of each piece of furniture and each appliance. Be sure to measure for any necessary top, bottom, or side clearances.

Also measure your rugs and rug pads. Write their dimensions in permanent magic marker on the undersides (or on masking tape attached to the carpet backing). You will use these measurements when you make out your floor plan.

Do all this before you begin your house-hunting trip. These measurements will come in handy when you are house-hunting. Bring these dimension with you to see if your rugs, pads, furniture, and appliances will fit in the homes you're considering.

While you are looking for a new home, measure the dimensions of each room. Once you have picked out your new home or apartment, you will have a physical record of each room, including window and door location and size, the locations of electrical outlets, heat ducts, fireplaces, etc.

With these room measurements, start planning your room arrangements. Draw the rooms to the same scale as your furniture template on pieces of graph paper (one room per page). Then, using your furniture template, draw in your furniture and appliances. Arrange and rearrange your furniture as often as you like on paper until you come up with a layout that you like.

When you move into your new home, simply tape each room's floor plan on its respective door. As each piece of furniture is brought in, you will be able to place it in its proper location the first time, putting an end once and for all to the games of musical chairs and sofas and dressers that so many people have played so often.

If you are using movers, your floor plan will be particularly useful. Once movers have loaded your goods on the moving vans, use your floor plans to record on your copy of the inventory sheets the room in which each item should be placed. At your destination, before they start unloading your shipment, show the movers around your house, point out the floor plans taped on each door, and explaining that you want the furniture placed exactly where indicated.

This will save your hours of frustration and manual labor. Even if you have never used movers, you can imagine how confusing it can be as movers, with sweat dripping off their foreheads, stagger in the front door and say: *Number 473. Where do you want it?* Instead of getting flustered and trying to guess the best place for that item, you simply consult your inventory sheets and your notes about where each item belongs.

A mover will put each piece of furniture where you want it, but only once! If you take the time to follow the above steps, you will cut down or eliminate the frustrations of furniture arranging and rearranging. You'll have more time and energy for unpacking and settling in.

If drawing, templates, and graph paper are not your cup of tea, take a look at the many computer programs on house design and remodeling. Some are easier to use than others, but all of them will help you plan your furniture arrangements.

Whether you do it by hand or on the computer, if you take the time to make your floor plans prior to your move, you will save a great deal more time and labor when you move in.

Appendix B

House-hunting Checklist

Address:

Agent:

Asking Price:

____ Lot Size
____ Square Feet
____ Rooms
____ Stories

____ Age of House
____ Property Taxes
____ Garage/carport

(Use margin for comments)

Yard:

____Usable size
____ Fenced?
____ Landscaped?

____ Well-lighted?
____ Patio/Terrace
____ Porch/Deck
____ Driveway

____ Sidewalks
____ Other

(Use margin for comments)

**Structure
and Exterior:**

General Condition:

Frame Description:

Exterior Description:

Foundation:

Roof Type, Age,
    Condition:

Gutters, Downspouts:

Doors, Windows,
    Screens, Storms:

Insulation and
    Weatherstripping:

Flooring:

Moisture or
    Water Problems:

Driveway, Sidewalks,
    Patio:

(Use margin for comments)

Neighborhood:

Streets:

Condition of Neigh-
    boring Property:

Sewers, Flood Control:

Noises, Visual Impacts,
    Bad Odors:

Zoning:

Nearest Industrial
Zoning:

Garbage Collection:

Street Lighting:

Traffic:

Proximity to:
____ Work
____ Schools
____ Shopping

____ Fire/Police
____ Public Transit
____ Highways
____ Hospitals
____ Parks
____ Recreation
____ Place of Worship
____ Other

(Use margin for comments)

Utilities:

Typical Utility Bills:
____ Gas or Oil
____ Electricity

____ Water and Sewer
____ Other

____ Municipal Water
or Well?

____ Sewer or Septic?

(Use margin for comments)

Interior

Room	size	closets	windows	outlets	carpet	comments
Living Room	____	____	____	____	____	
Dining Room	____	____	____	____	____	
Family Room	____	____	____	____	____	
Den or Library	____	____	____	____	____	
Entry or Hall	____	____	____	____	____	
Master Bedroom	____	____	____	____	____	
Bedroom 1	____	____	____	____	____	
Bedroom 2	____	____	____	____	____	
Bedroom 3	____	____	____	____	____	
Bedroom 4	____	____	____	____	____	
Master Bath	____	____	____	____	____	
Bathroom 1	____	____	____	____	____	
Bathroom 2	____	____	____	____	____	
Bathroom 3	____	____	____	____	____	
Laundry Room	____	____	____	____	____	
Breakfast Nook	____	____	____	____	____	
Garage	____	____	____	____	____	
Workroom/Shop	____	____	____	____	____	
Basement	____	____	____	____	____	
Attic	____	____	____	____	____	
Other	____	____	____	____	____	

	size	cabinets	counters	outlets	storage	comments
Kitchen						

Appliances:

____ Refrigerator	____ Disposal	____ Water Softener
____ Stove	____ Dishwasher	____ Air Conditioner
____ Microwave	____ Washer	____ Dehumidifier
	____ Dryer	____ Other Appliances

(Use margin for comments)

Plumbing:

____ Type	____ Water Pressure	____ Water Heater
____ Fixture Condition	____ Toilets/Drains	____ Capacity
____ Pipes	____ Leaks	____ Recovery time
	____ Sump Pump	

(Use margin for comments)

Electrical:

____ Wiring	____ 220 Volts?	____ Switches
____ No. of Circuits	____ Fuses or Breakers?	____ Outlet Availability
	____ Fixtures	____ Other Electrical

(Use margin for comments)

Miscellaneous:

____ Fireplaces	____ Wallpaper, Paint	____ Ventilation
____ Carpeting	____ Ceilings, Walls	____ Flooring
	____ Tile, Linoleum	____ Drapes, Curtains
	____ Lighting	*(Use margin for comments)*

APPENDIX C

Making A
Household Inventory

A household inventory is a written record of your personal property. It can be invaluable to you, not only when you move but whenever you need an account of your personal belongings. It will help you make sure that all of your property arrives at your destination. It will enable you to talk knowledgeably with insurance agents, financial planners, and anyone else who needs to know the nature or value of your property. And, if, despite all your precautions, an accident or disaster does happen, the inventory will make filing an insurance claim and reaching a final settlement much easier. The small amount of time you spend making and maintaining your inventory will be time well-spent.

There are many different ways to keep an inventory. Some people throw everything into a shoe box and trust that they will be able to find whatever records they are looking for. Others create a file of separate index cards for each item. Still others use a computer spreadsheet or database or purchase one of the many household inventory programs available. Some obtain inventory record forms from insurance agents, moving companies, or book publishers. (The publisher of this book has agreed to make reproducible inventory forms available at cost for readers who fill out the order blank at the back of this book.) Choose a method which works for you and one which you will use.

Decide in advance how you want to organize your records. Does it make more sense to arrange your inventory so that similar items are grouped together?

Or would you prefer to list items according to the room they are in? (To help you get started, see the lists of items and rooms to inventory below.) Some people find it easier to group items according to who is the owner of the item (Mom, Dad, Billy, Jill, etc.). It will be a lot easier to decide this before you begin than to change your mind half-way through the inventory.

The easiest way to begin is to go through your house or apartment room by room. Using the form of your choice, list each item of value. How much detail you include is up to you. The more information you have, the more descriptive your inventory will be. I recommend that you include enough information so you can answer any likely question about your property. Describe each item and how many you have if there are more than one. Include the make, model, and serial number. List where and when you bought it, what you paid for it, and (if appropriate) its present value and its replacement value. Indicate whether the item is personal or professional property.

Estimating the value of some items can be tricky. Have a professional appraisal of your collectibles and other items which can appreciate in value, such as antiques, artwork, rare books and coins, baseball cards, vintage wines, furs, or jewelry. Other items can probably be given a depreciated value according to IRS or insurance-company guidelines. If you have any questions about putting a value on an item, ask an insurance agent or financial planner for guidelines.

While you are taking your inventory of each room, use a camera or camcorder to make a visual record of your property. Photograph each item in its location and, if needed, from several sides. Open closet and cabinet doors to show their inventoried contents. If you are videotaping your property, narrate while you are recording, noting the room in which the picture is taken, the date of the filming, and the items you are inventorying. If you are using a still camera, write this same information on the back of each picture after the film has been developed. (Choose an ink which will not bleed through the paper and mar the photograph.)

When you are done with each room, go on to the next, repeating the inventory process until you have accounted for all your property. Don't forget to include the less-obvious areas of your home where you still may have property, such as garages, bathrooms, attics, closets, basements, or storage areas.

After all your property has been inventoried, gather your records together along with your inventory photographs and any supporting material such as bills of sale or professional appraisals. Your inventory won't do you much good if it is destroyed in a flood or fire that consumes everything on the list, so make copies of everything. Store one set of records at home and one outside the home in a safe deposit box, in your office, or at the home of a friend or a relative.

Update your inventory periodically. Whenever you add or dispose of a major item of property and whenever you move, make sure that your inventory is brought up to date. Once a year, if not more frequently, review the inventory to see if anything has changed. If so, revise your records accordingly. This may mean taking new photographs and having collectibles reappraised. (While you are at it, check to make sure your insurance coverage is still adequate.)

Items To Inventory

- Appliances—large (refrigerator, washer, stove, etc.)
- Appliances—small (blender, vacuum cleaner, garbage disposal, air conditioner, etc.)
- Books
- China and dishes
- Clothing
- Collectibles (antiques, baseball cards, artwork, etc.)
- Computer hardware (computer, monitor, printer, modem, etc.)
- Computer software (programs, games, etc.)
- Entertainment supplies (CDs, tapes, videocassettes, video games, etc.)
- Furniture and lamps (sofa, bed, table, mirror, etc.)
- Furs, jewelry, and accessories

- Glassware
- Hand and power tools
- Home electronics (stereo equipment, television, telephone equipment, clock, etc.)
- Lawn and garden equipment (lawn mower, barbecue, snow blower, etc.)
- Linens (towels, sheets, comforters, napkins, etc.)
- Memorabilia (photo albums, souvenirs, etc.)
- Musical instruments
- Photographic equipment
- Professional items
- Silver and flatware
- Sports and recreational equipment (golf clubs, treadmill, weights, etc.)
- Toys

Areas To Inventory

- Living room
- Dining room
- Kitchen
- Family room
- Master bedroom
- Other bedrooms
- Guest room
- Bathrooms
- Hallways
- Garage
- Work room
- Basement
- Study, den, library
- Office
- Yard, garden, pool
- Closets
- Attic
- Storage room
- Laundry room
- Porch, deck, sun room
- Drawers, files, cabinets, wardrobes, armoires
- Pantry
- Safe deposit boxes

Household Inventory Form

Date: _____

Room	Item, Model No., Serial No.	Where Purchased	When Purchased	Original Value	Present Value	Replacement Value	Cate-gory

APPENDIX D

Filing An Insurance Claim

Most of the time, moving goes smoothly. But occasionally things can go wrong. Moving is not always a gentle art. Accidents happen. Damage occurs. Things break. Shipments can be delayed or even lost.

If the unfortunate does occur, you will need to file a claim with the mover's insurance company or your own. This appendix includes a number of suggestions and tips for making claim filing as easy and straightforward as possible.

☐ Inspect your shipment for damages immediately. Put any damaged or destroyed items in one area. *Do not throw anything out*. A claims adjustor may insist on inspecting the damages prior to validating your claim.

☐ Notify your insurance company and the destination agent of the moving company immediately if damage or loss occurred.

☐ Get claim forms from the moving representative if you did not receive them upon the delivery of your goods.

☐ If you are paying for the move, ask your insurance company about the proper procedures for filing a claim.

☐ Even if the moving company's insurance is handling the claim, ask your insurance company also to inspect the damage.

☐ File a claim as soon as possible. You may have from six months to a year to file the claim, but the sooner you do file, the easier it will be to finish and the more quickly you will be reimbursed.

☐ Do not get anything repaired until the insurance company says it is okay. If your washer, dryer, refrigerator, or another necessity has been damaged, you must contact a claims adjustor first. The company normally will allow you to proceed with the repair before the claim is processed, provided that you furnish the company with an itemized receipt showing the exact damage and repair cost. If you have it serviced without permission, however, you may not be reimbursed.

☐ If large or expensive items are damaged, you will usually need to get estimates for replacement or repair. You may be advised to get your estimates from local stores which sell similar merchandise. If you need to pay for the estimate, be sure to itemize that expense on your claim form.

☐ Attach a copy of the Bill of Lading to all claims.

☐ If the delivery of your goods was delayed because of the negligence of the moving company, you can file an 'Inconvenience Claim.' You may be entitled to reimbursement for some of your living expenses during the delay. Keep all receipts for documentation.

APPENDIX E

Your 'Last Box'

Your last box should include all the items you will need to have available before the rest of your goods are unpacked. These are the basics which you normally use until the very last minute before you leave and which you usually need to use immediately upon arrival. It should contain some or all of the items listed in this appendix, as well as anything else which your particular situation demands.

Whether you are moving yourself or being moved, your last box should be placed where it can be unloaded right away. If you are using movers, instruct them to mark these boxes as *LAST BOX*, and make sure that they make a similar notation on the inventory sheets. When you or the movers are unpacking, place the last box where you will have unobstructed access to it.

Among the recommended 'last-box' items are:

☐ Coffee, tea, coffee cups, creamer, sugar, powdered drinks, instant oatmeal or cereal, cans of soup, peanut butter and jelly, crackers, raisins, and other convenient foods.

☐ Coffee maker or tea pot.

☐ A plastic pitcher.

☐ Paper plates, napkins, cups, paper towels, plastic silverware, and serving spoons.

☐ Pots, pans, a bottle opener, and a can opener.

☐ Bakeware.

☐ Food items.

- ☐ Trash bags, paper and plastic bags, aluminum foil, and plastic wrap.
- ☐ Dish soap and towels.
- ☐ Cleaning supplies, including rags, cleanser, window cleaner, and trash bags.
- ☐ Towels, sheets, pillowcases, pillows, blankets, shower curtain, bathtub mat, soap and shampoo.
- ☐ Toilet paper, tissue, paper towels, and napkins.
- ☐ A bag of screws, nails, hooks, etc.
- ☐ A screwdriver, a hammer, small tools, and scissors.
- ☐ Extension cords.
- ☐ A flashlight.
- ☐ A radio.
- ☐ A first aid kit and aspirin or acetaminophen.
- ☐ Clothes hangers.
- ☐ A phonebook from your previous hometown. (You will be surprised how many times you need this!).
- ☐ A few toys, books, and crayons.

APPENDIX F

Suggestions for Packing Your Car and Suitcase

Carry this book with you so it is always at your fingertips. It won't do you any good if it is packed in the box which ends up being the last one you unpack.

If you are flying, keep your luggage to a minimum. Airlines allow each person on domestic flights a total of three pieces of luggage, up to two of which can be carry-on bags. Any bag which exceeds a seventy-pound weight limit will have to go separately as air freight. If you are over either limit, mail a small box of items to yourself at your new address. (Save your receipt.)

International baggage limits will depend on the carrier and the country of destination. Be especially careful to find out and observe the weight limits if you are moving abroad. It is very expensive to mail anything overseas.

Carry your school records, medical and dental records, powers of attorney, wills, credit cards, vehicle documents, keys to your luggage (two sets), insurance policies (or copies of them), maps and itinerary, Social Security cards, drivers licenses, reservation and confirmation information, relocation information, a travel diary, passports, travel orders, vaccination records, pet shot record, mover inventory sheets and bills of lading, and a notebook to record daily expenditures.

Pack your jewelry and valuables, including coin and stamp collections, important papers (birth certificates, extra passport photos, etc.), photographs and appraisals of your high value items, money from childrens' wallets and piggy banks, photo negatives and other sentimental items that can't be replaced, family histories, heirlooms, etc. Do not leave these alone in a car unless it has an alarm. Keep your valuables with you at all times. To be safe, do not pack receipts, photos, or appraisals in the same box or suitcase as the items which they document.

Are you shipping your car? Carry the car's serial number, motor number, ownership papers, and an extra set of keys with you.

Keep in your possession a list of credit-card numbers and customer service phone numbers in case your cards are lost or stolen.

Also pack the following:

- ☐ Clothes, shoes, accessories, toilet articles.
- ☐ Extra checks.
- ☐ Blank health insurance claim forms.
- ☐ An address book with updated telephone numbers.
- ☐ Drivers manual for your destination state or country.
- ☐ Your 'good driver's certificate' if you are moving overseas.
- ☐ A first aid kit, prescriptions medicines, and aspirin or acetaminophen. Note that most doctors prefer acetaminophen (such as Tylenol®) over aspirin for anyone under the age of twenty. Aspirin has been associated with a condition known as Reye's Syndrome among young people. Check with your own doctor or pediatrician before giving any medications to children.
- ☐ Extra fuses, a fire extinguisher, and an emergency toolbox if you will be traveling by car.
- ☐ Sunglasses, an extra pair of eyeglasses, trash bags, travel games, books and magazines, snacks and drinks.
- ☐ If you are traveling with a pet: paper towels, room deodorant, scooper, plastic bags, water, food, bowls, a blanket, toys, and any medicines (such as motion sickness medication) which your veterinarian has prescribed.
- ☐ Items that movers will not ship (See Appendix F) and those you want to transport yourself.

(Note: if you are transporting open bottles of liquor, make sure they are in the trunk).

☐ A travel alarm clock.

☐ An umbrella.

☐ A camera.

☐ A travel iron and a sewing kit.

☐ Clothing appropriate for your destination.

☐ Office or work clothes, in case your suitcase is lost.

☐ Detergent for washing clothes en route.

☐ Baby things, including pins, bottles, food, clothes, diapers, etc.

☐ An electrical converter if you are moving overseas.

☐ A small box of tools and hardware for moving in (a hammer, a screwdriver, pliers, a wrench, nails, screws, three-way plugs, a tape measure, scissors, and other necessary items).

☐ Lightbulbs and matches.

☐ Extra batteries.

☐ Bathroom and personal articles.

☐ Toilet paper, tissues, and wet-wipes.

☐ A telephone. (You can plug it in as soon as you arrive if you have pre-arranged for telephone service.)

☐ Graph paper, template, furniture dimensions, and a plastic grid for finalizing your floor plans.

☐ 'Fanny packs' to use while sightseeing.

☐ Any birthday or anniversary cards you need to mail while en route.

☐ Wrapped gifts for new acquaintances and for friends along the way.

APPENDIX G

Items Which Movers
Will Not Pack

These are hazardous and other items which carriers are prohibited by law from transporting. They include:

- Paints.
- Flammables.
- Aerosol cans and pressurized containers including deodorant, shaving cream, hairspray, etc.
- Explosives.
- Matches.
- Fire extinguishers.
- Lightbulbs and florescent bulbs.
- Batteries.
- Nail polish remover.
- Open liquor bottles.
- Antifreeze.
- Shoe polish.
- Bleach.
- Chemistry sets.
- Propane gas.
- Lighter fluid.
- Candles.
- Cord wood.

NOTE: Guns can be moved as long as they have the bolt, firing pin, and trigger assembly disassembled. There are various state and federal laws you need to check. Overseas shipments are subject to individual country regulations.

APPENDIX H

Other Helpful Sources

Many moving companies and trailer rental companies are excellent sources of information about destinations and moving in general. Even though I have moved more times than I want to remember, I have always found the information these companies make available to be very useful and informative. Some make video tapes available for a nominal deposit. Many agencies have information racks in their waiting rooms. Many others make literature available by request from their central offices. (HINT: Whenever you request information or literature, always include a self-addressed, stamped envelope.)

Government Publications

Your Rights And Responsibilities When You Move, Interstate Commerce Commission, Rm. 4133, Interstate Commerce Commission Building, 12th St. and Constitution Ave., N.W., Washington, D.C. 20423 (202-927-5500).

United States Department of Education, *Choosing a School for Your Child,* Consumer Information Center, Pueblo, CO 81009. (Send a stamped, self-addressed envelope.)

Useful Books And Pamphlets:

American Movers Conference, *Guide to a Satisfying Move* (American Movers Conference, 2200 Mill Road, Alexandria, VA 22314).

Henry Constantino, *Moving? Don't be Taken for an Expensive Ride* (Mission Viejo, CA: Transportation Publishing Co., 1988).

L. Robert Kohls, *Survival Kit for Overseas Living* (Yarmouth, ME: Intercultural Press, Inc., 1984).

Denise Lang, *Phantom Spouse: Helping You and Your Family Survive Business Travel or Relocation* (Whitehall, VA: Betterway Publication, Inc., 1988).

Lee and Saralee Rosenburg, *50 Fabulous Places to Retire in America* (Hawthorne, N.J.: The Career Press, *1991*), and *50 Fabulous Places to Raise Your Family* (Career Press, 1993).

George Sullivan, *Do it Yourself Moving* (New York: MacMillan Publishing Co., Inc., 1974)

Special Resources For Military Moves

USAA Foundation, *Moving with the Military* (The USAA Foundation, USAA Building, San Antonio, TX 78288-0028).

American Forces Information Service, *It's Your Move* (Dept. of Defense, 1987).

"Moving," The Times Magazine (Army, Air Force, Navy Times Publishing Co., June 18, 1979), 33-37.

Overseasmanship (NAVPERS 15314). For members of the military.

Special Resources for Moving with Children

Home is Where My Heart Lives: A Workbook for Children on the Move (Enterprise Services International, Inc., 16 Horner Street, P.O. Box 718, Warrenton, VA. 22186; $18.00 plus $4.50 shipping). This is a workbook for helping children express their feelings when their family moves.

Books of Related Interest
from Silvercat Publications

✓ **THE TRAVEL HEALTH CLINIC™ POCKET GUIDE TO HEALTHY TRAVEL**, by Lawrence Bryson, M.D. (ISBN 0-9624945-4-2, $13.95)

Guidelines for traveling safely and staying healthy on the road by the medical director of San Francisco's Travel Health Clinic.

✓ **THE COUNTRY CLUB: WHY SWITCHING FROM THE BIG CITY TO THE BOONDOCKS COULD BE YOUR SMARTEST MOVE EVER**, by Dale Wildman (ISBN 0-9624945-5-0, $8.95)

Practical tips and frank, useful advice and encouragement about moving to the country from an author who has lived in both places.

Please send me :

___ copies of *Moving: A Complete Checklist and Guide for Relocation*, at $8.95 each.

___ copies of *The Travel Health Clinic Pocket Guide*, at $13.95 each.

___ copies of *The Country Club*, at $8.95 each.

❑ I am enclosing a check for _____. (California residents please add 7.75% sales tax. There is no charge for handling or postage.)

❑ Please add me to your mailing list. I am particularly interested in books about:

Name _____

Title _____

Company _____

Address _____

City_____ State, Zip _____

Order from:

Silvercat Publications
4070 Goldfinch St, Suite C
San Diego, CA 92103-1865
(619) 299-6774